Lilli Gore is British by birth, Austro-Hungarian by
parentage and 'French by inclination'. Her favourite part of
Europe is the Var in Provence. She writes that 'there on
the hills covered with thyme, juniper, rosemary and
uncountable other delicate herbs, birds and beasts feed,
thereby giving their flesh a unique flavour. It seemed the
natural place to write a book about game cooking, inspired
by both the *chasse* and the cuisine which in those parts
have a gusto not encountered in the more seda.. areas
where hunting is permitted.'

Between writing about food and travel she is collecting
material for an encyclopedia on cooking utensils and
kitchens.

Game Cooking

LILLI GORE

Illustrated by M. J. Mott

PENGUIN BOOKS

Penguin Books Ltd,
Harmondsworth, Middlesex, England
Penguin Books,
625 Madison Avenue, New York, New York 10022, U.S.A.
Penguin Books Australia Ltd,
Ringwood, Victoria, Australia
Penguin Books Canada Ltd,
41 Steelcase Road West, Markham, Ontario, Canada
Penguin Books (N.Z.) Ltd,
182–190 Wairau Road, Auckland 10, New Zealand

First published by Weidenfeld & Nicolson 1974
Published in Penguin Books 1976

Copyright © Lilli Gore, 1974

Made and printed in Great Britain by
Hazell Watson & Viney Ltd,
Aylesbury, Bucks
Set in Linotype Juliana

To Georgiana and David

CONTENTS

8   Game Cooking

Fur

ACKNOWLEDGEMENTS

I should like to acknowledge my indebtedness to the many cookery books which I consulted when preparing this book. They refreshed my memory and directed my researches into new fields of inquiry.

Outstanding among these valuable and pleasurable books were *A Highland Cookery Book* by Margaret Fraser, *The Finer Cooking* by Marcel Boulestin, *Cocina regional española*, *Good Poultry and Game Dishes* by Ambrose Heath, *La Veritable Cuisine provençale et niçoise* by Jean-Noel Escudier, *Madame Prunier's Fish Cookery* edited by Ambrose Heath, *A Concise Encyclopedia of Gastronomy*, compiled by the late André Simon. In addition I also consulted *Plats du jour* by Patience Gray and Primrose Boyd, *Mrs Beeton's All about Cookery*, *The Gourmet Cookbook*, *La Physiologie du goût* by Brillat-Savarin, translated by Anne Drayton, *The Epicurean* by Charles Ranhofer, *Larousse gastronomique* by Prosper Montagne, *French Provincial Cooking* and *Italian Food* by Elizabeth David, and *What We Eat Today* by Michael and Sheilagh Crawford.

To these authors and to all those friends whose cooking has extended and enriched my experience of the art I acknowledge my indebtedness and offer my thanks. I would also like to thank my daughter Georgiana who compiled the index.

Lilli Gore

INTRODUCTION

This is a book about *real* food, not plastic food. When I wrote the first edition of this book I didn't know that my instinctive feeling about the goodness of game had been confirmed by scientific research. At the Nuffield Institute of Comparative Medicine it has been discovered that, as its director, Dr Michael Crawford, says in his book *What We Eat Today*, 'The carcass from an animal free to select its own food [e.g. game, L G] produces three times as much protein as adipose fat; the carcass of an intensively reared animal produces three times as much adipose fat as protein ... intensive high energy production is providing the community with adipose fat not protein.' So far game has managed to avoid the grotesque indignities inflicted on many creatures to increase their production.

But between 1973 and 1975 the UK exported (mainly to the EEC countries) 12,442 tons of game meats (excluding the offals). This earned approximately £8,542,934 in assorted foreign currencies – hardly an important contribution to the balance of payments particularly when set against the high price of imported protein foodstuffs. Perhaps we could buy game more cheaply and find more butchers willing to sell it if its export were discouraged. Although I understand the need of some people and the desire of others to have their deep-freeze stocked with foods in and out of season I personally find the idea slightly nauseating. For the charm of the first ripe strawberries or fresh salmon is a kind of recreation of childhood's treats – too many of them and the stomach rebels.

Just as the flavour of game varies from place to place its sheer seasonality is another of its main attractions. I freely admit to prejudice and as far as the deep-freezing of other foods is concerned I prefer not to enter the controversy as to whether the nutritive value, the texture or the flavour are adversely affected. So far as game is concerned I am convinced that it is better eaten freshly killed than deep-frozen. It is food to cook with pleasure, not heat up for convenience.

Game is beautiful. You cannot can it, dehydrate it or factory-farm it successfully. In a plump game bird, you can taste the memory of the fragrant woodlands and fresh fields from which your bird flew. Of game, the famous gastronome Brillat-Savarin said : 'It provides most of the full-flavoured dishes which constitute trans-cendental cookery.'

Considering the rapturous praise which game has inspired there are surprisingly few books devoted exclusively to its cooking. To define our field briefly : game is 'any wild animal, bird or fish commonly hunted for sport as well as food'. The range is wide. The thirty-five million hunters and fishermen of America would number grey squirrels, black bear and moose in their bag. High communist officials of central Europe take to the dark forests in pursuit of wild boar. For practical reasons this book will be confined to those birds, animals and fish which are most often classified as game the world over.

The killing of most types of game is strictly controlled in Britain and the times of the various open seasons are given in the appropriate sections.

In the United States there are also strictly enforced laws which vary from state to state as to the times of the hunting seasons both for small and large game. There is also a limit on the size of the bag for all types of game which in principle belongs to the state, not to the owner of the land. In general the shooting season for small game and birds lasts from 1 November to 14 February. Big game hunting begins on 1 December and goes on until February at the longest and the end of December at the shortest, depending on the state.

There are four main categories of game in America, small game, which includes the rabbit, the hare – also known as the Jack rabbit or Snowshoe rabbit – the furcoat-bearing muskrat, the squirrel, the opossum, and the woodchuck.

Big game is abundant; the most widespread are the various members of the deer family, including the elk and the moose. The buffalo, which at one time was in danger of extinction, now flourishes on the western ranges. (I don't know whether the buffalo meat sandwich I ate in a San Francisco delicatessen was hunted or farmed, but it was quite delicious.) Prize game is the bighorn sheep and the bear. The Russian boar, imported into the United States early in the twentieth century, obviously unaffected by the fluctuations in political relations, flourishes in the Tennessee mountains. It also is a coveted proof of the huntsman's skill.

Upland game in general covers the members of the pheasant, partridge, quail species, the woodcock and the dove.

All areas in the United States contain some kinds of waterfowl; among them wild duck, geese and snipe.

Unlike the other categories of game, waterfowl shooting is controlled by Federal Law, but both State and Federal bodies are responsible for their proper maintenance. Strict conditions are in force as to the methods by which they may be shot and also as to the quantities taken.

It is almost impossible to know what percentage of the sportsman's bag or catch ever gets into the shops – this applies equally to Great Britain as to the United States. Generally the American butcher will buy his game from a game farmer, where animals and birds are bred in conditions similar to their wild state. Although this does not fit very closely with the concept of game being hunted for food and sport, a reasonable similarity to their natural habitat is likely. Equally important to the sportsman is the fact that the game-farms release their surplus stocks into the countryside, replenishing these natural stocks in danger of extinction from pollution and other causes.

Game birds, unlike poultry (with which cookery books usually lump them), are seasonal. They are usually at their best between mid August or September and about the end of February. This coincides pleasantly with the autumn and winter, when hot food is more welcome, and when cooks do not grudge time spent in the kitchen. For, leaving aside the hunter's extemporized kitchen or the hastily organized barbecue, game cooking does need some time and forethought.

Game, unlike poultry again, will vary in flavour, depending on its feeding grounds. The rabbit that lives on the wild thyme and rosemary of Provence will differ from his corn-fed American counterpart. Such individuality is part of the distinctiveness of game.

There is sure to be a wide age range in any game bag, and subsequently in the shops. There are fairly simple broad indications of the age of game birds and animals. The surest signs of youth in birds are the pliability of beak, feet and skin, and in both animals and birds plumpness of breast and brightness of eye. Bright eyes are your guide to your game's freshness too.

However, from a practical point of view, it is simpler to rely on the evidence of the supplier or donor as to age. It will not take long to find out if the game-dealer is knowledgeable as well as honest.

It is important to *know* whether you are buying a young or elderly animal, as the preparation and cooking times vary so much. Equally important is the length of time that it has been hung.

The optimum time for hanging is one of the more disputed gastronomic aspects of a subject already fraught with controversy. The notion that a pheasant is only fit to eat when it is so 'high' that the weight of the bird, hung by its legs, will make it drop as the flesh putrefies, 'drawing out the legs', is, to say the least, unattractive. Four days to a week hanging satisfies the majority of palates, while, if it is not hung at all, the flavour is not appreciably different from chicken.

Another myth, that game is invariably expensive, can now be exploded. In fact hare, rabbit, pigeon and venison are weight for weight as cheap if not cheaper than many other kinds of meat or poultry (always excepting the battery hen). In certain years pheasant and partridge are also relatively cheap.

Restaurants, however, do charge a great deal for game. Few have game on the menu. Few of those that do deserve the price they put on it. If dining out is pleasant as a way to eat dishes you cannot create at home, then serving your guests with game at home is doubly worth the enterprise.

There is good evidence that game has always been highly prized. Emperors and wealthy Romans dined or were fêted with prodigious quantities of game – seven thousand game birds formed part of the feast given for Vitellius on his triumphal return to Rome. In the

Middle Ages, the hunt played an important part in the Court's activities. Strict laws were enforced to keep the forests as preserves for the king, and the chase and killing of an animal were accompanied by a strict ritual. Gargantuan quantities of food were served at our ancestors' celebrations; at a feast given by a medieval archbishop the items included 500 roe and buck, and 1,500 hot pasties of venison.

Quantity, not quality, was the rule. Such great French chefs of the eighteenth century as Soyer and Carême (who had fled from the Revolution) demonstrated the subtleties of game cookery. But our guzzling grandfathers preferred bulk. With Edward VII came breakfasts with woodcock and cold grouse, lunches of game pies, and twelve-course dinners to finish.

Today, the time is right for rediscovering the true pleasures of game. I wrote this book in a farmhouse of Provence, the air balmy with wild thyme. Friends, too numerous to mention by name, from America and England have refreshed my memory of their own favourite and personally tried recipes. But finally I have drawn on my own experience of cooking game at home, in Spain and central Europe and London. I offer you fair game in the hope you will find as much delight in it as I have.

Mrs Nourse's recipe for roast pike, which begins, 'Clean the fish nicely, make a forced meat thus: take a good deal of bread-crumbs, minced parsley ...' without going into details of quantities, is really all that should be necessary for the 'professed' cook. But *Modern Practical Cookery* by Mrs Nourse, published in 1813, from which the extract has been taken, was in fact intended for non-professed cooks. It seems probable that we non-professed cooks could be somewhat perplexed by her instructions.

Consequently, I have included details of quantities and timing. They are not intended to be taken as exact scientific rules, since ovens, like taste, are idiosyncratic. Equally those flavours delicious to me may be anathema to others.

The quantities are intended for four average appetites, unless otherwise stated. My own inclination is always to cook too much rather than just enough.

Some recipes are very familiar, others less so. They were selected from a variety of sources: some were told to me, others I watched being cooked, many came from books I have used for years. A few which I could not resist, are well-known gastronomic, virtuoso pieces, almost fantasies.

The recipes in general proceed from roast game, poached in the case of fish, to the more elaborate dishes, simply because those ways of cooking very often form the first part of an operation, not because I think it is easier to produce a perfect roast partridge.

Although I have tried to be as practical as possible, occasionally, like many cooks and lovers of food before me, I have been carried away. But if so restrained and classical a painter as the eighteenth-century Claude could say that there were only two arts, 'painting and ornamental pastry', I am in good company.

WHAT THEY ARE

BOUQUET GARNI

A small bunch of herbs to flavour food cooked in liquid or steam. Basically parsley, thyme, and bay leaf.

BROTH/STOCK

The liquid in which meat, fish, vegetables, or all three, are cooked; the basis of sauces, jellies etc.

CROÛTONS

Slices of bread fried or grilled in butter or other fat; in rounds to support small game birds; cut into various shapes as garnishes.

SALMIS

Roast game, carved and finished in a rich stock and wine sauce.

ZEST

The thin, coloured, outside layer of the peel of citrus fruit.

COOKING TERMS

BARD

This is to cover game or pieces of game or meat and less often fish with a thin slice of fat – either salt pork, streaky bacon or pork fat. The bard prevents the meat drying out, especially the breasts of small game birds. The bard, which should be large enough for this purpose, is tied on with string.

BASTE

To keep food moist by pouring its stock or other liquid over it while it is braising or roasting.

BOIL

The bubbling of liquid which is just about to vaporize.

BONE

To remove the bones from a bird or small animal, while keeping the flesh and skin intact, so that its original shape can be reconstructed with stuffing.

BRAISE

To cook with very little liquid in a closely covered pan. The food is usually browned first in fat.

BROWN

This means either to brown the fat – butter for example, or to cook the food until it is brown.

BUTTER

To rub softened butter over a pan or dish to prevent food from sticking.

CHOP

To cut into tiny pieces with a chopper or sharp knife. Mince in USA.

CLARIFY

To clear stock or remove solids from butter.

DEEP-FRY

To cook in hot fat which completely immerses the food.

DICE

To cut into very small cubes.

DRAIN, DRY

To remove food from liquid or fat; in the latter case the food is placed on absorbent kitchen-paper. Dry, for meat or fish is to pat dry with a cloth or absorbent paper.

DREDGE

To cover by sprinkling or dipping food into flour or sugar or any other finely ground substance.

FILLET

To cut the flesh of fish off the central bone before cooking, also thin slices cut from the breast or saddle of game.

FLAME

To ignite warm alcohol poured over food – the alcohol evaporates but the flavour remains.

FOLD

To amalgamate a light, fluffy mixture, e.g., whipped egg whites, with other food, so that the air remains enclosed.

FRICASSÉE

To stew or braise with a white or pale sauce.

FRY

To cook in a small quantity of hot fat.

GALANTINE

A dish made from meat, poultry, or fish served in its own jelly.

GARNISH

The decoration of trimming added to a main dish.

GLAZE/DEMI-GLAZE

To produce a shiny surface on food. Fish or meat may be glazed with a gelatinous concentrated stock, either under intense heat or with aspic jelly. Vegetables are glazed by cooking in butter and sugar.

GRATIN

To brown and make a crisp coating on the surface of food, either under the grill or in the oven, by sprinkling it with breadcrumbs, butter, sometimes cheese, or all three.

GREASE

To rub the surface of a dish with any kind of fatty substance.

GRILL / BROIL

To cook by exposing the food to direct heat.

JELLY

Originally a clear meat or fish stock, which solidifies when cold because of its gelatinous constituents. Now usually made with gelatine. A preserve made from fruit, its juice and sugar.

JUG

To braise in a casserole, as in jugged hare.

LARD

To lubricate meat with strips of fat (lardoons) pulled through the flesh with a larding needle. To make deep cuts in the meat and push the lardoons into it.

MARINADE

For tenderizing, lubricating and flavouring. This liquid is known as the 'marinade'.

MARINATE

To steep any meat or fish in a mixture of herbs, vegetables and spices, wine or other liquid etc.

PAPILLOTE, EN

To finish cooking in greased paper cases so that all the juices stay inside.

POACH

To cook in hot liquid which is simmering so gently that it just trembles.

POT ROAST

To cook in a covered pot on top of the stove.

POUND

To make a paste of food traditionally with a pestle and mortar, but other suitable utensils can be used.

REDUCE

To evaporate water from a stock or sauce to increase the flavour and thicken it.

ROAST

To cook in the oven, by dry heat, or on a spit.

SAUTÉ

To fry quickly in a small quantity of fat.

SCORE

To make regularly spaced light cuts with a sharp knife.

SEAR

To prevent juices of meat escaping by intensive heat.

SIEVE

To force vegetables or fruit through a strainer to make a purée.

SIMMER

To cook in a liquid in which bubbles never break at the surface, because the temperature remains just below boiling point.

STRAIN

To separate liquids from solid food sometimes through a tammy cloth.

SKEWER

To push a skewer through to keep meat or bird in shape.

TRUSS

To tie or fix the legs and wings of a bird or animal close to the body with string and/or skewers.

WHISK OR BEAT

To force air into a substance e.g. egg whites or cream by beating with a whisk or other utensil.

COOKING MEDIA – BASIC METHODS

Batter for Deep Frying

As a coating for deep frying a flour-based batter is adequate, but the food must be eaten immediately it is cooked. Fine matzo meal makes a crisper batter than flour.

¼ lb. sifted flour or matzo-meal, pinch salt, 1 egg, ¼ pt milk.

Mix the seasoned flour with egg to form a thick paste. Stir the milk in little by little to prevent the mixture getting lumpy. Beat with a whisk till it froths; leave to stand before using.

Beurre Manié

Kneaded butter is a thickening for gravies, stock and sauces used in the actual cooking. Knead the butter and flour together to a paste. Add little bits, the size of a pea, to the boiling liquid and stir. Cook until the sauce thickens. It is the principle of the roux in reverse.

1 oz. flour to ¾ oz. butter approximately, or 1 heaped tbs. of flour to ¾ oz. butter.

Clarified Butter

Cut up the pieces of butter to be clarified into small pieces. Melt them in a saucepan over a moderate heat. When it begins to froth remove the foam and strain the liquid through a fine muslin into a bowl. Cover and keep in the refrigerator. Ideally, all meats should be fried or sautéed in clarified butter as there is very much less chance of burning. The residual solids may be used in sauces.

Court Bouillon

Traditionally a mixture of water and wine or wine vinegar, or lemon, combined with flavourings such as celery, carrots, onion or shallots and a bouquet garni, and seasoning of salt and pepper. This liquid is simmered gently for 30 minutes. Fish bones and trimmings added make a fish stock.

3 tbs. each chopped onions and carrots to 2 pts water. Crushed clove of garlic and bouquet garni plus wine to cover fish completely.

Fumet of Fish, Game

A very rich concentrated essence made by reduction of the original game or fish stock.

Panada

This is a paste made of a starchy substance such as flour, bread, potato, rice, with milk, stock or water, for binding forcemeat of either fish or meat. The proportion of panada to the basic ingredients is 1 part panada to 2 parts of the other ingredients. A bread panada is made by soaking the bread or breadcrumbs in milk and cooking it on a fierce heat stirring all the time. When the paste is quite smooth and ceases to stick to the spoon or the sides of the pan it is ready. Spread it on a plate and let it *cool* before using it – it is most important to let it cool.

A Frangipane panada is made with flour, egg yolks and butter, as follows:

3 oz. flour, 3 egg yolks, 2 dessertspoons melted butter, pinch salt, 1 pt milk.

Boil all the ingredients over a hot fire until they make a thick paste. Allow to cool before using.

The Frangipane panada is very similar to choux pâté.

Roux, white, blond (pale), brown

Roux are the bases of innumerable thick sauces. The white roux is flour mixed with butter over heat and cooked for just long enough with liquid to destroy the flavour of uncooked flour.

Blond roux is the same mixture of heated butter and flour cooked so that it just changes colour.

Brown roux is the flour and butter cooked together until it has become a light brown and smells nutty. It must be cooked slowly or else the flour will burn.

White Sauce

This is a basic sauce to which a great variety of flavourings may be added depending upon the dish for which it is intended. If the sauce is meant to coat the food, the proportions of flour and butter to liquid should be reduced by ½ oz.

3 oz. butter, 3 oz. flour, 1 pt milk/stock, salt, pepper (in this case, white).

Add the flour to the hot fat and stir and gradually add the stock/milk (it is possible to use half of each). Stir all the time the liquid is being added, which will prevent it becoming lumpy. Bring to the boil and simmer for 3 or 4 minutes.

TEMPERATURES AND MEASURES

Oven Temperatures

These temperatures are those which are roughly equivalent to the different ovens of the ordinary domestic cooker.

For slow cooking, like braising or stewing, the temperatures may be slightly higher or lower without making any appreciable difference. Slight variations in temperatures will be more crucial in the timing of small roast game.

Equivalent Oven Temperatures

Electricity °F	°C	Gas No.	Solid Fuel
240–310	116–54	¼–2	Slow
320–70	160–88	3–4	Moderate
380–400	193–205	5	Fairly Hot
410–40	210–19	6–7	Hot
450–80	232–49	8–9	Very Hot

Cup Measures

American cup measures are smaller than the British standard cup. Below are some equivalents between tablespoons and ounces and British and American measures.

Abbreviations for quantities

tbs.	tablespoon
tsp.	teaspoon
oz.	ounce
1 glass	1 wine glass (6⅔ fluid oz. approximately)
1 small glass	a liqueur glass approximately
1 tumbler	½ pint

One ounce (approximately)	*Level tablespoonfuls*
Breadcrumbs, dry	3
Butter, lard (soft enough to press into bowl of spoon)	2
Flour, unsifted	3
Gelatine, powdered	2½

Other Measures

1 American teaspoon (tsp.)	approximately ⅙ oz.
1 American tablespoon (tbs.)	3 tbs. or 1 fluid oz.
16 American tablespoons (tbs.)	1 American cup

An American tablespoon holds exactly ¼ oz. flour, measured level.
1 American cup holds 8 fluid oz. or ½ American pint (English or Imperial ½ pint or cup equals 10 fluid oz.).

CONVERSION TABLE

Liquid Measures

British

1 quart	=	2 pints	=	40 fl. oz.
1 pint	=	4 gills	=	20 fl. oz.
½ pint	=	2 gills or 1 cup	=	10 fl. oz.
¼ pint	=	8 tablespoons	=	5 fl. oz.
		1 tablespoon	=	just over ½ fl. oz.
		1 dessertspoon	=	⅓ fl. oz.
		1 teaspoon	=	⅙ fl. oz.

Metric
1 litre = 10 decilitres (dl) = 100 centilitres (cl) =
1000 millilitres (ml)

Approximate equivalents:

British	Metric	British	Metric
1 quart	1·1 litre	35 fl. oz.	1 litre
1 pint	6 dl	18 fl. oz.	½ litre (5 dl.)
½ pint	3 dl	9 fl. oz.	¼ litre (2·5 dl)
¼ pint (1 gill)	1·5 dl	4 fl. oz.	1 dl
1 tablespoon	15 ml		
1 dessertspoon	10 ml		
1 teaspoon	5 ml		

American

1 quart	=	2 pints	=	32 fl. oz.
1 pint	=	2 cups	=	16 fl. oz.
		1 cup	=	8 fl. oz.
		1 tablespoon	=	⅓ fl. oz.
		1 teaspoon	=	⅙ fl. oz.

Approximate equivalents:

British	American	British	American
1 quart	2½ pints	1½ pints + 3 tbs.	1 quart
1 pint	1¼ pints	(32 fl. oz.)	
½ pint	10 fl. oz. (1¼ cups)	¾ pint + 2 tbs.	1 pint
¼ pint (1 gill)	5 fl. oz.	(16 fl. oz.)	
1 tablespoon	1½ tablespoons	½ pint − 2 tbs.	1 cup
1 dessertspoon	1 tablespoon	(8 fl. oz.)	
1 teaspoon	⅓ fl. oz.		

Solid Measures

British	Metric
16 oz. = 1 lb.	1000 grammes (g) = 1 kilogramme (kilo)

Approximate equivalents:

British	Metric
1 lb. (16 oz.)	450 g
½ lb. (8 oz.)	225 g
¼ lb. (4 oz.)	100 g
1 oz.	25 g

British	Metric
2 lb. 3 oz.	1 kilo (1000 g)
1 lb. 2 oz.	½ kilo (500 g)
9 oz.	¼ kilo (250 g)
4 oz.	100 g

UTENSILS

BAIN-MARIE

A wide shallow pan for keeping sauces warm by surrounding them with hot water; also for cooking terrines in the oven.

BASTER

A metal tube with a rubber bulb on one end.

BRAISING PANS/CASSEROLES

Heavy metal pans or fire-proof dishes which spread heat evenly. Oval-shaped pans are more suitable for game birds and fish.

CHERRY OR OLIVE STONER

A spike on the top half pushes the olive or cherry pip through the hole on the other side of this gadget.

CHOPPING BOARD

As large as is convenient and at least one inch thick.

CHOPPING BOWL AND CURVED KNIFE

A small wooden bowl and knife whose curve fits the bowl. Ideal for chopping fresh herbs.

CONICAL SIEVE

For straining sauces a conical sieve is invaluable.

DEEP FISH-FRYER

Safer and more effective for deep-frying fish, rabbit etc.

FISH KETTLE

Oval saucepan with a strainer to lay fish on.

FISH SCALER

Like a grater – from Sweden.

HINGED MOULD

For removing a pastry covered game pie easily.

KITCHEN SCISSORS

For trimming fish, game, birds, bacon etc.

KNIVES

3 sharp ones are the minimum. A small one for peeling and boning, medium for slicing, and large for chopping.

LADLE

For removing small quantities of stock or other liquids.

LARDING NEEDLE

The thick end grips a thin sliver of fat to pull it through the flesh of bird, joint or animal.

MANDOLIN

An oblong wooden board 12 inches long with a variety of adjustable blades fixed in it for slicing vegetables very thinly.

MOULINETTE

A mini-mill for vegetable purées.

PEPPER MILL

For grinding peppercorns quickly.

PESTLE AND MORTAR

For pounding fish or meat and crushing spices, garlic etc.

POULTRY SHEARS

Curved blades for jointing game birds and poultry.

ROASTING PAN AND RACK

Big enough for a brace of pheasants; the rack stops the flesh burning.

SPATULA

For folding egg whites, cream, etc into a mixture.

SPOONS

For stirring, mixing and measuring.

TAMMY CLOTH

Cone-shaped cloth for straining sauces.

WHISK

For beating mayonnaise, egg whites, cream and sauces etc.

Feather

Preparation of Game Birds

Plucking

Pluck the bird somewhere where a few feathers flying about will not matter. The first lot of feathers can be plucked over a large bag or bucket. Remove the smaller wing and tail feathers first, then finish plucking on a hard surface or a board. Pluck from the tail towards the head without damaging the skin. If the skin is frail, pluck from head to tail. For tough wing feathers use a knife or tweezers; if the quills break pour boiling water on the wings and the feathers will come out easily.

Drawing

To remove the sinews from older birds, make a lengthwise slit in the leg just above the claw, to expose the sinews. With a skewer hooked under each sinew, pull them out one at a time. Cut off the feet at the first leg joint. Cut off the head about 2 inches from the body. Pull down the skin towards the body and cut off the neck as close as possible. If the skin of the neck is cut down a little way, it is possible to loosen the wind-pipe and gullet. With a sharp pair of scissors or a knife, cut round the vent and slit the skin so that there is enough room to get the fingers inside the body cavity. Take hold of the gizzard (stomach) and pull out all the entrails. Keep the giblets (gizzard, heart and liver) and fat. Finally, wipe the inside with a clean, damp cloth.

Singeing

Singe birds carefully by holding them over a gas flame or use a long taper. Wipe the bird hard with a damp cloth and remove any quills that remain.

Trussing (truss *after* stuffing)

With the exception of woodcock and snipe, game birds are trussed the same way; either with a trussing needle and fine string or skewers and string. Fold the skin of the neck over towards the back and the tips of the wings backwards, so that they hold the skin in position. Lay the bird breast upwards and press the legs as close to the body as possible. Slit the skin above the vent (parson's nose) and push it through the slit. Push the threaded needle (or skewer) through between the wing joints, and do the same with the legs just above the parson's nose, so that the fleshy part is not pierced. Tie the ends of the string. The idea of trussing is to make a compact parcel which makes cooking and carving easier.

Giblets

The gall bladder must be cut away from the liver without puncturing it; if any of the flesh has been in contact for any length of time with the gall it will be too bitter to eat. Clean the gizzard by cutting in two and peel off the inner membrane and contents. To make stock, the cleaned feet, head and wing tips may be added to the giblets.

Boning

Boning game birds for a galantine or ballotine: cut off the feet, neck, and end joints of the wings. Start the boning at the neck. With a small, very sharp knife work as close to the bone as possible and separate the flesh from it. In order to bone the wings, cut through from the inside at the point where they join the body. Cut along the bone, scraping away the flesh from it, turning it inside out. Repeat from the other side for the other wing. Continue down the body and deal with the legs in the same way as the wing.

Grouse

Gastronomes may argue for ever about the relative merits of grouse, pheasant or partridge, but one thing is certain – the true grouse (in the culinary sense) is unique to the British Isles. It is bred successfully only in Scotland, Yorkshire, other parts of northern England, the West of Ireland and Wales. The 'Glorious Twelfth', which one might think was the name of an army regiment, is in fact the date on which strangely-clad men take off for the moors and the grouse. The first grouse of the season is to the British gastronome what the first glass of the Beaujolais d'année is to the French. For on 12 August the first (legitimate) grouse is shot, and probably airlifted to the most expensive restaurants in London, to appear on the plates of those who have been unfortunately deprived of the ritual shooting.

Although grouse is in season from 12 August until 15 December, those shot between mid August and mid October and bred in that year, are the most succulent. Young birds have soft downy feathers on the breast and under the wings, which should be pointed. Young grouse respond best to simple cooking – roast or grilled – but older birds can still be delicious if cooked slowly. But there is almost nothing tougher than a really old grouse. Grouse is equally good eaten hot or cold. In general, a young grouse is only enough for one, but as they mature between October and December, one will be just enough for two people.

Traditional accompaniments to roast grouse include breadcrumbs fried in butter, gravy, rowan jelly, or more commonly red-currant jelly and bread sauce. Some, to my mind, unwise cooks serve all of these as well as game chips and watercress garnish. If you are going to serve roast grouse on croûtons then there's no need for the breadcrumbs, but the tart jellies are in order, and the watercress looks good and is nice and crisp to munch. If you *need* to serve gravy with roast grouse then the grouse has been badly cooked – the pork fat or bacon bards should have kept the breast moist. Rowan jelly is as good with roast grouse as cranberry is with turkey, but it is fairly difficult to come by. The mountain ash which grows wild on the moors provides the best fruit. Strangely enough, it seems to have disappeared from suburban gardens where you used to see it often; killed by pollution perhaps?

Scottish recipes include skirlie, which is a pleasant change from the more usual garnishes of breadcrumbs. The basis of skirlie is oatmeal : to 2 oz. of butter or beef dripping add 2 chopped onions and brown them. Add 2 oz. of oatmeal and cook very gently for about ten minutes, while the oatmeal absorbs the fat and onion juice.

Grouse may be hung from two days to a week, but only the condition of the bird, that is its fatness, the weather and personal taste can say what length of time is best. A good dealer will describe his birds as either young or casserole grouse. The most important thing about cooking older grouse is that it *must* be marinated and *slowly and gently* cooked.

A MARINADE FOR GROUSE

Warm 3 tbs. of olive oil, add a sliced onion and carrot; 1 clove of garlic, 4 crushed juniper berries, bouquet garni, 2 glasses red wine, salt and pepper.

Simmer for 20 minutes, let it cool and pour it over the grouse. Marinate for a minimum of 4 hours.

Recipe

Roast Grouse

4 young grouse, 4 oz. butter, salt and pepper, 2 tbs. red berries (e.g. red-currants, cranberries or rowan berries) or lemon juice, 4 slices mild bacon or salt pork fat, grouse livers, flour, 1 tbs. olive oil, 1 oz. butter, 4 slices white bread.

Mix 3 oz. of the butter with the berries, or, if not using berries, soften with the lemon juice; season with pepper and salt and put a knob inside each bird. Tie the fat securely around the birds and wrap them in foil. Roast in a hottish oven (no. 6) for about 25 minutes, breast-down on a rack in a pan. Fry the livers in the remains of the butter and then mash them. Five minutes before serving, remove the foil and fat from the grouse, dredge the breasts with seasoned flour, and brown. Serve on croûtons fried in the olive oil and butter and spread with the mashed livers.

Alternatively, the bread can be put in the roasting pan to absorb the cooking juices before spreading with the mashed livers. A garnish of watercress may be served. If the birds have been stuffed with red berries it seems superfluous to serve any red berry jelly: however, if the butter has been flavoured with lemon juice then serve with the jelly.

Grilled Spatchcocked Grouse

4 very young grouse, 4 oz. butter, pepper, salt, 1 tsp. dried marjoram, (optional 4 tbs. white breadcrumbs). For the garnish of maître d'hôtel butter: 1 tbs. chopped parsley, lemon juice, 1 oz. butter.
4 slices white bread, 1½ lb. mushrooms.

Split the grouse down the back and put a small skewer through the base of the legs to keep them flat while cooking. Melt the butter, add pepper, salt and marjoram, and brush the grouse on both sides with this mixture. Cook under a medium hot grill for 20 minutes in all, turning the birds over occasionally but basting frequently with the melted butter mixture. About 10 minutes before the grouse are cooked, place the trimmed slices of bread under the grill rack. Grill the mushrooms and serve the grouse on the bread, which should have absorbed the cooking juices and be crisp and brown. Place a pat of maître d'hôtel butter (see p. 171) on top of each bird Serve with the mushrooms.

The grouse can also be grilled with a coating of fine white bread-crumbs, but should be cooked more gently, so allow another 5 minutes or thereabouts for cooking.

Pot Roast Grouse

2 grouse, 4 oz. butter, 1 cup rich stock, 1 glass wine, sherry, vermouth, or brandy, pepper, salt.

Brown the grouse in the butter in a heavy pan. Season, and add the stock and wine. Cover tightly and cook in a slow oven (no. 3) for about 1–1½ hours, until tender. Serve with mashed potatoes and cranberry sauce.

Braised Grouse

2 grouse, ¼ lb. fat bacon diced, 2 cups stock, 1 or 2 carrots sliced, 1 sliced onion, 2 sticks celery, pepper, salt, bouquet garni, 1 clove garlic. (If other juicy vegetables, like tomatoes, are added use less stock.)

Brown the grouse in the bacon fat. Remove grouse, and gently sauté the vegetables; add the garlic and bouquet garni and stock. Place the grouse on top of the vegetables and cook slowly for about 2 hours. Serve on rice or mashed potatoes.

Grouse Salmis

2 grouse, 2 thin slices salt pork fat, grouse livers, 1 glass dry wine, 1 cup rich meat stock, 1 finely chopped shallot, 2 lemons, ¼ lb. mushrooms, 1½ oz. butter, 1 tbs. flour, 2 tbs. chopped parsley, pepper, salt, and 2 sprigs of thyme.

For a salmis the birds may be half cooked for the first part of the operation either by roasting or sautéing. Bard and roast the grouse in oven (no. 5) for about 20 minutes, or until half cooked. Alternatively, sauté them. Cut them up into serving pieces on a dish in which you are going to mix the sauce, so that the blood which oozes out when you carve can be used. Keep the grouse on one side in a shallow casserole. Mash the livers in the dish with the grouse juices, the wine, stock and juice of both lemons, chopped shallot, and season with pepper and salt. Mix well and pour over the grouse pieces. Put the sprigs of thyme and sliced mushrooms into the casserole, cover and cook gently for another 15 minutes on top of the stove. Stir occasionally to prevent the grouse sticking. Thicken with the beurre manié before serving. Serve on rice, mashed potatoes, or purée of turnip.

Cold Grouse

2 small cooked grouse, 1 lettuce, 4 tomatoes, 2 hard-boiled eggs, watercress, 2 uncooked eggs, 2 tbs. olive oil, 2 tbs. vinegar, 1 tbs. parsley, a shallot or a small Spanish onion.

Cut the grouse in pieces, serve them on a lightly seasoned salad made with the lettuce, tomatoes and quartered eggs. Make a sauce of the 2 well-beaten egg yolks mixed with the olive oil like a very thin mayonnaise, add the tablespoon of chopped parsley and the shallot or onion. Season with salt and pepper. Alternative salads to serve with cold grouse are endive, orange or mixed green salad.

Grouse Pudding or Pie

1 grouse, 1½ lb. topside beef, 2 tbs. flour, 1 large onion sliced, garlic, 2 carrots sliced, bouquet garni, 2 oz. beef dripping, ¾ pt stock, ½ lb. short-crust pastry or suet pastry (see p. 164).

Cut up grouse and beef into largish chunks, sprinkle all these with the flour, and fry with all the vegetables in the beef dripping in a heavy pan. Add the stock and cook slowly until almost tender on top of the stove with the lid on the pan.

For a pudding: line a pudding basin with the suet pastry, cover with a cloth and steam for about one hour.

For a pie: put the grouse and vegetables into a pie dish. Cover with the pastry rolled out to ¼ inch thick; put a pie funnel in, brush the pastry with beaten egg and cook for 5 minutes in a hot oven, lower the heat and cook for another 25 minutes.

Grouse en Cocotte

2 grouse, 1 oz. butter or dripping, 2 diced carrots, 2 onions, 1 turnip, 1 stick celery, ½–¾ pt jellied stock (see p. 17), bouquet garni, 1 glass red wine, 1 dessertspoon red-currant or rowan jelly, 32 very small onions.

Marinate the grouse for 4 hours in the marinade (see p. 33). Wipe the grouse, and brown them slowly on all sides in a heavy stewpan in the butter, take them out and keep aside. Add the vegetables, cover with a lid and brown them. Place the grouse on the vegetables, season with salt and pepper, add the bouquet and enough stock to cover all the ingredients. Flambé the wine in a small saucepan and pour it over the grouse. Cover the pan tightly and cook slowly on top of the stove for 1½ hours. Baste occasionally during cooking. Remove grouse, put them on a serving dish, split them down the middle. Strain the cooking liquid and reduce it to a thick syrupy consistency. Season to taste, add jelly, and spoon over the grouse. Serve with the glazed button onions (see p. 162).

Grouse Stew

Unless grouse are cheap to buy, this dish is best left to those households where grouse is plentiful.
1 or 2 grouse, marinade (see p. 33), ¼ lb. diced bacon, 1 sliced carrot and onion, bouquet garni.

Marinate the grouse overnight. Drain and dry the grouse. Sauté them in a casserole for 15 minutes with the bacon. Strain the marinade over it. Add carrot, onion and fresh herbs and cook very slowly with the lid on for at least 2 hours. If extra liquid is needed during cooking add some hot water.

Terrine of Grouse

2 grouse, 1 glass brandy, 8 rashers of mild bacon, ½ lb. finely minced pork, 1 cup stock, 1 clove garlic crushed, 2 tsp. salt, pepper, 1 tsp. thyme.

Carve the breasts of the grouse into fillets, and as much flesh off the rest of the grouse as possible. Fry all the meat gently. Leave the fillets to marinate in the brandy while you pound or mince the rest of the flesh with the livers. Mix the pork and pounded grouse together, season and add the thyme. Line a fire-proof dish or tin with the bacon rashers and fill it with alternate layers of the fillets, forcemeat and bacon, finishing with the bacon. Pour the stock with the crushed garlic all over. Cover closely and cook in a bain-marie (see p. 27) for 1½–2 hours in a moderate oven (no. 4) with a piece of foil over the terrine and then a lid. The terrine is cooked when the juices are just clear fat, yellow without any traces of pink. Remove the terrine from the water, take off the lid and place a round plate or rectangular tin, whichever fits into the terrine, on top and a weight on top of that. Cool the pâté with the weight on and then refrigerate. Serve cold with a salad, green or otherwise.

Potted Grouse   Useless .

2 grouse, casseroled or stewed, ½ lb. melted butter, ground mace, and a pinch of cloves.

Cook grouse as in recipe for grouse stew (p. 37). When the grouse are tender, drain the cooking liquid off completely. Skin the birds and remove all the flesh from the carcass, discard the gristle and tendons. Cut the flesh into strips. Fill small pots or terrines with tightly packed layers of grouse, each layer being covered with the melted butter seasoned with the ground mace and cloves. Finish with the melted butter. In the refrigerator these potted grouse will keep for some weeks. They make an excellent hors d'oeuvres, or lunch. Serve with a salad.

Partridge

Your true British bird ... the plump delicate partridge ... not your 'coarse red-legged French infantry' as Major Pollard calls it, is said to be the finer eating. However, there are red-legged partridges in Essex and Hertfordshire and grey partridges as far east as the Dnieper in White Russia. Other species abound in the United States and Asia. But legend has it that they were originally introduced into Provence for breeding in the fifteenth century by King René of Naples.

The common or grey partridge of Great Britain is particularly plentiful in arable farming areas like East Anglia, but it can be found in all parts of the United Kingdom. Although it lives mainly on corn, the birds like to have gorse, scrub and hedges for cover near by.

Partridge is in season from 1 September to 1 February, but they are at their best in October and November. A young partridge can be recognized by the rounded tip of its first flight feather and the yellow brown of its feet. The average weight of partridges varies from the young at ¾ lb. to 1½ lb. for a mature, but not necessarily elderly bird. The hen is thought to be a shade more tender than the cock so when they are bought in a shop a brace (pair) usually consists of a hen and a cock, so that all the customers get fair shares.

Only young partridges should be roasted or grilled, and they must be well lubricated with fat. Old birds can be equally good, if not more delicious, casseroled, braised or made into salmis.

A good plucked partridge should have light-coloured flesh, almost no bones and a plump breast; at the optimum age for eating, say between two and four months, it will weigh about a pound.

For four people a young partridge apiece is usual as a main course, but two older birds may be enough for four. The average time for roasting is twenty-five to thirty minutes and for slow cooking, two hours.

Depending on the weather and personal taste, a partridge should be hung from the neck, unplucked and undrawn, in a cool airy place for from two to five days.

Traditional accompaniments to roast partridge are watercress salad or garnish and game chips, or fried breadcrumbs.

Roast Partridge (1)

2 young partridges, 8 vine leaves, 2 thin slices of bacon or salt pork fat, slices of white bread.

Blanch the vine leaves if they are the kind preserved in brine. Wrap each partridge first in the vine leaves and then in the fat, tied on very securely. Roast them in a hot oven or on a spit for between 20–25 minutes. Serve on croûtons of fried bread; garnish with watercress and game chips. Serve with endive and orange salad.

Roast Partridge (2)

A brace of partridge, 4 oz. butter, 2 slices of salt pork or mild bacon, flour, 2 slices bread, salt and pepper, ½ glass red wine, a dessertspoonful red-currant or quince jelly.

Place seasoned lump of butter in each bird, tie on the bard securely, and roast in oven for about ½ hour (no. 5–6), basting often with melted butter. When practically ready remove the bard, sprinkle flour on, baste and leave to 'froth', i.e. brown. Serve on moistly fried bread, with a sauce made from the pan juices, to which a spoonful of jelly and the red wine have been added.

Roast Partridge (stuffed)

To the purist, roasting a partridge with anything more than a knob of butter inside it may seem heresy. All the same, the following stuffings help to keep the partridge moist, and are nice to eat, without noticeably affecting the delicate flavour.

STUFFING (1)

The partridge livers, 1 cupful breadcrumbs, pepper, salt, 1 tbs. chopped onion, 1 oz. butter.

Mix together and stuff the partridge.

STUFFING (2)

2 or 4 young partridge livers, ¼ lb. chopped ham, ¼ lb. mushrooms, 8 juniper berries, black pepper, 4 oz. butter, 4 thin slices pork fat.

Mash the partridge livers and mix these together with the ham, mushrooms, and finely crushed berries, and black pepper. Stuff the partridge with either mixture and secure the slices of pork fat when trussing. Roast the birds for 25–30 minutes in oven (no. 5), basting frequently with melted butter. Place them on a serving dish when cooked and keep hot. Meanwhile, fry the slices of bread in the fat accumulated in the roasting pan. Serve with the fried bread and endive salad. Omit fried bread for partridges stuffed with breadcrumbs.

Grilled Partridge

2 young partridges.

These can be cooked slowly under the grill in the same way as grouse (p. 35), or pigeon, or marinaded first in an oily marinade. Cook about 10 minutes either side, basting and turning them over once or twice during cooking.

Grilled Spatchcocked Partridge

2 young partridges.

Split the partridges carefully down the back so that they lie flat. Spread with softened butter. Grill gently for 10 minutes either side. If desired cover with white breadcrumbs and brown under the grill. Serve with a sauce diable or périgueux (see pp. 168 and 172).

Grilled Partridge with Mushrooms

2 young partridges, 4 oz. butter, salt and pepper, juice of ½ lemon, ½ lb. mushrooms.

Split the partridges down the back so that they lie flat while cooking. Spread them thickly with the butter and cook under a medium-hot grill for about 20 minutes in all. Turn at least twice during cooking and baste very often. Add the salt and pepper to the melted butter for basting. About 7 minutes before the partridges have finished cooking, place the mushrooms under the grilling rack and let them cook in the mixture of butter and cooking juices. Serve on a very hot dish with mushrooms. Game chips and watercress make a nice combination of textures with the succulent partridge and mushrooms.

For a change, dip the buttered partridges in fine white breadcrumbs mixed with finely chopped parsley. Cook a little longer and more slowly to allow heat to penetrate the gratin. Alternatively, add the breadcrumbs halfway through the cooking. Serve with quartered lemons.

Poached Partridge

2 plum young partridges, 8 vine leaves (see p. 39), 4 thin slices of mild fat bacon, salt and pepper.

Wrap each bird in the vine leaves first, then in the bacon, securely tied on. Poach them, completely covered in boiling water, for about 40 minutes. Remove vine leaves and bacon. Eat with croûtons and red-currant jelly and a bowl of young broad beans.

Cold Poached Partridge

Follow the recipe for poached partridge above, but plunge them into iced water until they are quite cold. Remove all the wrapping. Serve on lettuce salad. A revelation for all those who think that the best flavour of young partridge is only attainable by roasting.

Partridge Poached in Creamy Milk

1 or 2 partridges (since this dish is more suited to an older partridge, it is possible that one partridge will be enough for four people), 2 pts rich creamy milk, 1 large onion stuck with 1 or 2 cloves, 2 sticks celery, 2 carrots, salt and pepper, bouquet garni with a sprig of tarragon or ½ tsp. dried tarragon, 1 oz. flour, 1 oz. butter for beurre manié (see p. 22).

Truss the partridge and put it in a saucepan so that the bird is entirely covered with the milk and the added onion, carrots, celery, herbs and seasoning. Poach it slowly with the lid on for 3 hours. About 15 minutes before serving, remove a pint of the milky stock and add the beurre manié to thicken it. Remove the partridge on to a serving dish, carve it into serving pieces. Serve the sauce separately with a tablespoonful of chopped parsley in it. Delicious with purée of spinach or Jerusalem artichokes.

An alternative to poaching in milk is to cook the partridge in a chicken or veal stock flavoured with onion, celery, herbs, salt and pepper. Cooked this way the partridges are delicious eaten cold with a vinaigrette dressing, or sauce verte (see p. 173).

Partridge and Apples

2 young partridges, 4 very thin slices of pork fat or unsmoked streaky bacon, 4 oz. butter, salt and pepper, ½ tsp. marjoram, a pinch of nutmeg, 1 lb. eating apples, small glass calvados, 1 cup thick cream, 1 tsp. lemon juice.

Bard the partridges and brown them on all sides in half of the butter. Use a shallow heavy pan so that the partridges fit fairly tightly into it. Season with salt, pepper and a generous pinch of marjoram and a sprinkle of nutmeg. While the partridge is browning cook the apples very gently in the rest of the butter in a small enamel saucepan for about 5 minutes. Add them to the partridges and simmer on top of the stove for 30 minutes with the lid on. If the partridges are not tender enough by this time and the apples look as if they are drying out add a little more hot water. When the birds are tender take them out and put them on to a heated serving dish, remove the fat slices and flambé the birds with a small glass of calvados (for preference) or brandy. Into the pan, with the apples and cooking juices, pour the cream and bring to the boil gently. A teaspoon of lemon juice added just before pouring it all around the partridges adds a judicious touch of tartness to the flavour. The point of using eating apples is that cooking apples, while providing the tartness, are too watery for this dish.

Partridge with Cabbage

4 partridges, 4 rashers bacon diced, 1 large carrot and onion sliced, 4 small onions, 4 cloves, 4 thin slices pork fat, 2 small cabbages coarsely cut, bouquet garni, ½ pint stock (preferably game stock), salt, pepper, 1 glass white wine.

Put the bacon, carrot and onion into a heavy metal casserole. Spike the small onions with one clove each and put an onion into each partridge. Tie the pork fat when trussing the partridges. Cover the vegetables with a good thick layer of cabbage and place the partridges on top of it with the rest of the cabbage covering them. Put in the bouquet garni, pour the stock over it and season well with salt and pepper. Cook slowly on top of the stove with the lid on for

$2\frac{1}{4}$ hours. Five minutes before serving, add a glass of white wine. Put the partridges on a hot dish on a bed of the cabbage, carrot and sliced onion. Strain the remaining gravy, boil and pour over the partridges. Most people prefer to remove the onion stuffing when they untruss the birds before serving. This dish is often served with sausages or pork added to the cooking at appropriate times. With the addition of all these and boiled potatoes it becomes a very substantial dish, but rather less partridgy.

Partridge à l'Espagnole

4 partridges, 4 bacon rashers, 4 tbs. olive oil, 2 cloves garlic, 2 large onions, 2 carrots, 1 tsp. salt, $\frac{1}{2}$ tsp. pepper, $\frac{1}{2}$ bottle red wine, $\frac{1}{2}$ pt water, $1\frac{1}{2}$ oz. chocolate.

Retain liver and heart of dressed partridges. Slice carrots and onions. Bard partridges, brown in olive oil with garlic, onions and carrots, and add liquid. Simmer for $1\frac{1}{2}$ hours. Remove partridges to a serving dish and keep them warm. Fry livers and hearts and chop them finely : melt the chocolate in a greased cup and mix with the giblets, add to the sauce, boil and simmer for a couple of minutes. Pour over the partridges and serve.

Partridge with Grapes

Casserole the partridges (see p. 47).

Before serving, add a small bunch of about 30 seedless grapes, a small cup of rich stock and 1 or 2 tablespoons of burnt cognac. Simmer closely covered for about 10 minutes. Serve in the same dish it was cooked in.

Partridge en Papillotes

2 young partridges, 4 oz. butter, 1 tbs. oil, pinch marjoram, oregano, salt, pepper, 1 tsp. each grated orange and lemon rind. Greaseproof paper or foil.

Cut the partridges in two from top to bottom and sauté the pieces in butter for 10 minutes; season them with freshly ground pepper, salt, a pinch of oregano and marjoram mixed, grated lemon and orange rind, and let them cool. Take as many pieces of greaseproof paper as you have halves of partridge (4 in this case). Make sure they are big enough to completely cover the half of partridge with enough paper left at the edges to prevent the steam escaping. (Stapling the edges together is a rather neat way of doing this.) Grease the paper with a mixture of oil and butter and put a thin slice of bacon on each. Lay the pieces of partridge on the paper, fold the paper over and fix the edges together. Lay them on the rack in a roasting tin and cook in the oven for 15 minutes on no. 5. Garnish with watercress and serve with gooseberry or other tart jelly and sauté potatoes.

Partridge with Sour Cream

2 youngish partridges, 2 thin slices fat bacon, 3 oz. butter, 4 rashers unsmoked lean bacon diced, 2 sliced carrots, 1 cup sour cream, ½ tsp. paprika, salt, pepper, juice of ½ lemon, 1 glass white wine.

Soften 1 oz. butter with some lemon juice, season with salt and pepper, and put a lump inside each bird. Wrap the fat firmly round each bird. Place them on top of the bacon and carrots in a shallow covered pan. Cook in a moderate oven for 30 minutes basting frequently. While the partridges are roasting, melt the chopped shallots and onion in the rest of the butter, add the wine and reduce by about half. Take the partridges from the oven, remove the fat slices and place the birds and the vegetables on a fire-proof serving dish. Keep warm in the coolest possible oven. To the melted onions and shallots add the sour cream and a good pinch of paprika. Reduce this sauce so that it thickens but does not become a purée. Pour over the partridges. Serve with rice, potatoes or buckwheat.

This is a simple method of cooking a mature partridge, but it does need constant watching to make sure the partridge is absorbing the stock and flavouring but is not getting dry.

Stewed Partridge

1 large partridge, 12 small onions, 2 sprigs thyme, 2 bay leaves, a sprig of fresh basil if possible, 2 cloves garlic, 2 pts stock.

Truss the partridge and put it into a deep saucepan which just fits it. Cover it completely with a rich stock, seasoned with the salt, pepper, herbs and garlic. Cook it very gently with the lid on for 4 hours, so that all the stock evaporates very slowly. Add the glazed onions and take the lid off and brown the partridge. Serve with a poivrade sauce (see p. 172).

Try half cider and half stock as a variation on this dish.

Braised Partridge

4 young partridges, 4 oz. butter, 1 sliced carrot and onion, ¼ tsp. dried or sprig of fresh thyme, 1 bay leaf, salt, pepper, 2 glasses red wine, 4 rashers streaky bacon, 1 tbs. flour, 1 cup cream.

Sear, without burning, the trussed partridges and vegetables in the butter in a large heavy pan, for 10 minutes. Add the thyme, bay leaf, salt and pepper and 1 glass of wine; reduce the heat, cover the pan and simmer for 40 minutes. Add the bacon and second glass of wine, cook for another 25 minutes, adding if necessary a little hot water if all the liquid appears to be evaporating. Take the tender birds out and keep hot on the serving dish. Add the flour very gradually to the liquid left behind in the pan so that it thickens. When all the flour has been absorbed strain the sauce into a small pan. Pour in the cream. Untruss the birds and pour the sauce over them. Serve with a purée of lentils (see p. 47) or turnips sprinkled with chopped parsley.

Partridges in Sweet–Sour Sauce

4 partridges, 4 rashers fat bacon, 4 sliced shallots, 1 sliced carrot, bouquet garni, black pepper, 2 tsp. brown sugar, 1 tsp. flour, 1 glass red wine, 1 tbs. capers, juice of ½ lemon.

STUFFING

1 lb. coarsely chopped mushrooms, or ½ lb. mushrooms and ¼ lb. mild ham chopped.

Cover the bottom of a large casserole with the bacon, shallots and carrot, and place the stuffed partridges on top. Add ½ pt cold water, 1 bouquet garni and a generous sprinkle of black pepper. Simmer for 1½ hours or more (depending on the age of the birds).

When they are tender, keep them hot on a serving dish. Dissolve the sugar in the gravy, stirring it constantly to prevent burning. Stir in the flour very gradually and then the wine, little by little. Lower the heat and add the lemon juice and capers. Raise the heat again and let it bubble for 10–15 minutes: untruss the partridges, take out the stuffing and surround the birds with it. Pour the sauce over the birds and serve with sauté or mashed potatoes.

Casseroled Partridges with Lentils

2 partridges, 2 oz. butter, 1 medium-sized onion sliced, 2 carrots sliced, 1 glass white wine, 1 cup rich stock, ½ lb. brown lentils, 1 onion, 1 clove garlic, 1 bay leaf, pepper, salt.

Truss the cleaned partridges and lightly brown them with the vegetables in the butter in a pan into which the birds fit quite tightly. Add the wine and reduce it by a third, then pour in the stock. Add seasoning. Simmer very gently for at least 2 hours with the lid on. The lentil purée can be made while the partridges are cooking, or in advance. Cover the lentils, onion, bay leaf and garlic with water, add seasoning and simmer for 1½ hours. Make sure the lentils are soft. Drain them, remove the bay leaf and make a purée either in a blender or a moulinette, or by putting them through a sieve. Add 2 tablespoons of the sauce from the pan to the lentil purée in a small saucepan, and heat on a gentle fire. When it is evenly mixed with the sauce put it on a warmed serving dish. Place the partridges in the centre and pour the remainder of the sauce over them to serve.

For those who prefer lentils whole (as I do) prepare the lentils by boiling in the same way as for a purée. Mix them with 2 large sliced Spanish onions gently fried in 2 tablespoons of oil, 1 oz. butter, 1 clove garlic. Serve with chopped parsley. An endive or crisp lettuce salad is all that is needed to accompany this filling dish.

Both old and young birds respond to this method of cooking – but the young ones will need only half the time of cooking in the oven.

Stewed Partridge in White Wine

4 young or old partridges, ¼ lb. fat pork cubed, 2 glasses white

wine, bouquet garni, 1 clove crushed garlic, salt and pepper, 1 cup stock, 1 oz. butter, 1 small glass brandy.

Melt the pork cubes in a heavy pan and when the bottom of the pan is covered with fat put the partridges in breast upwards. Flame the brandy and pour it over the partridges. Turn the birds breast-side down and pour in the wine. Let this come just to the boil. Add the bouquet, crushed garlic, salt and pepper and the stock. Keep the steam in by putting foil between the lid and the pan. Cook in a low oven (no. 3) for 1½ hours. When the partridges are tender, remove them on to a serving dish. Strain the gravy into another saucepan; reduce this by half. Add 1 oz. butter and let it all melt until it looks glazed. Pour over the partridges. Serve with a purée of peas, brown lentils or turnips.

To try when hiring a villa in Spain, but not for traditionalists of partridge eating. Old partridges are best for this dish which will take at least 2 or 3 hours to cook. Young birds will take about half this time.

Partridge with Orange and Garlic

2 large or 4 small partridges, 2 oz. pork fat, 2 tbs. flour, 2 glasses white wine, water, pepper and salt, 2 thinly sliced red peppers, 2 unpeeled sliced oranges, 12 (24) peeled garlic cloves.

Truss partridge and brown in a heavy saucepan with pork fat; add the flour gradually and brown that as well. Pour in the 2 glasses of wine and enough water to bring the liquid to reach halfway up the partridges. Season with pepper and salt. Cover and simmer on a low heat for 1–1½ hours depending on the age of the partridges. Now add the pimentos. While the partridges are cooking, boil one sliced orange in 1 pint of water. At this point those who prefer their garlic somewhat muted can also boil the garlic cloves for 10 minutes; this water *must* be thrown away. Add the orange slices, the liquid, the garlic, and the juice of the second orange. Cook the partridges for another hour. When tender remove them and keep hot. If it is necessary, thicken the sauce by reducing it.

If you can get them, Seville oranges are marginally better for this dish, but first blanch them. Serve with garlic, peppers and orange.

Cold Braised Partridge

2 partridges, pepper, salt, 4 oz. butter, 2 rashers of chopped bacon, 1 chopped shallot or onion, small glass rum, juice of 1 lemon.

Season the birds well with salt and pepper and truss and bard them. Place them in a heavy pan and braise on top of the stove on medium heat in 4 oz. butter for 1½–2 hours, with the lid on. When they are tender cut them in halves lengthwise and put them on a dish. Pour over them 4 tablespoons of good rum and the juice of ½ a lemon. Cover the dish and leave for 8 hours. Turn them over occasionally. Serve cold on beds of lettuce hearts with a little vinaigrette sauce made with oil and lemon.

Salmis of Partridge

4 partridges, 1 lb. fat bacon diced, 2½ oz. butter, 2 chopped shallots, salt, pepper, 1 tbs. fresh chopped thyme and basil (or ¼ tsp. mixed dried), 2 oz. sliced ham, 1 glass red wine, preferably claret, juice ½ lemon, 1 tbs. flour.

Make the stock with the giblets beforehand if possible. Brown the partridges in a large frying pan or sauteuse in the butter with the diced bacon for 15 minutes. Turn them during cooking so that all the parts brown evenly. Remove the partridges from the pan; as soon as they are cool skin them and carve, cut the breast into fillets and then if possible cut off the flesh from the legs. Chop the carcasses into small pieces and add the skin. Put these in a saucepan with the shallots, pepper, salt, ham and herbs. See that all the ingredients are covered by the stock (if not, add some water). Simmer for 1½ hours. Remove any fat (with kitchen paper), add a glass of red wine. Put the pieces of partridge back in this sauce and warm gently, keeping it simmering. Do not let it cook too fast as the partridge may get tough. While the partridge is reheating make a brown roux with ½ oz. butter and ½ oz. flour, and enough of the sauce to bring it to the right consistency. Put the pieces of partridge in the middle of the serving dish and pour the sauce over it.

Instead of claret, port may be used and the sauce may be flavoured and thickened with red-currant jelly. Serve with triangles of toast.

Partridge Pâté, Terrine (See Terrine of Hare and Rabbit, pp. 127, 140)

The weight of partridge, that is the total weight of the bird dressed but uncooked, should be roughly equal to the other meat, say pork or veal, or a mixture of both. Partridge is less strong than hare in flavour so more delicate seasoning should be used. If anything, pâtés and terrines tend to be too strongly seasoned, so start by under-seasoning.

Chaud-froid of Stuffed Partridge (See Chaud-froid of pigeon, p. 66)

It is worthwhile taking all the bones out because partridges are somewhat bigger than, say, pigeon or quail.

Pheasant

The pheasant is delicious, beautiful and of mysterious origin. The Romans with their *dolce vita* habits are supposed to have brought the pheasant to Britain, but this 'bird of Phasis' as its Latin name, Phasianus, suggests, was first known by the river Colchide, which separated Europe from Asia.

'It is an enigma to which only experts have the key, and they alone can savour it in all its excellence,' said Brillat-Savarin – fortunately a wild exaggeration.

Despite the fact that it is the only game bird hand-reared and almost hand-fed, it has never been domesticated, and in some strange way has retained the flavour of wild game. Its diet consists of a variety of berries, fruits, bulbs, nuts, grass and so on.

All pheasants have two features in common; their long beautiful tails and their red-wattle rimmed eyes. They are shot from 1 October to 1 February, but their season of excellence from November to January is too brief for 'custom to stale it'. Young pheasants of both sexes have soft feet and light plumage; the cock has rounded short spurs; the first wing-tip feather is pointed in a young bird and rounded in an old one. Hens are better to eat than cocks, which are easily recognized by their iridescent feathers and more beautiful curving tails, and in shops they are usually sold in pairs – a brace.

A pheasant must be hung to develop its distinctive flavour; the length of time will vary with weather and personal taste, from four to seven days is the average time. If the bird is not hung at all it will be tougher than a chicken and with no appreciable difference in taste.

A roasting pheasant weighing two pounds may be enough for three people but an older bird can feed four. Only young birds should be roasted or grilled and they should be barded with thin slices of fat over the breast and rubbed with butter inside. Old birds improve with barding too in dishes where sautéing is a preliminary stage in the recipe. Old pheasants can be cooked in much the same ways as partridges, and go very well with a variety of fruit or vegetables in the cooking.

The average time for roasting a pheasant is about forty-five minutes, for braising or other slow cooking, a minimum of two hours.

Use only very young birds – two may be enough. If so, adjust the quantities of other ingredients accordingly.

Recipe

Roast Pheasant

4 young pheasants, salt, pepper, 4 oz. butter, 4 thin mild bacon rashers.

Having trussed the birds, season them well inside and out. Secure the bacon slices, spread butter generously all over. Roast breast down in a hot oven (no. 7) for 20–25 minutes according to the size of the bird. Five minutes before they are ready remove the bacon slices, dredge the breasts with flour, return to the oven with breasts upwards to brown. Serve with a garnish of watercress and a tart red jelly like red-currant. Fried breadcrumbs, game chips, brussel sprouts are alternative accompaniments – but one at a time. Gravy or Madeira (see p. 171) or bread sauce (see p. 167) are alternatives which can also be served.

The tail feathers stuck back in their original position makes a fine Fellini-like entrance.

Roast Pheasant with Onions

4 young pheasants, 4 slices bacon, 4 oz. butter, 4 shallots or 4 small Spanish onions, salt, pepper, flour, cooking foil.

Tie on the bacon and put 1 oz. butter and a shallot or small Spanish onion inside each bird. Season well inside and out and wrap each bird in foil. Lay the birds breast down on the roasting rack and cook in oven (no. 7) for ¾ hour or longer if necessary. Remove the foil, taking care to see that all the fat and juices go into the roasting pan, dredge the breasts with flour, return to the oven and brown, basting once or twice with the fat. Serve as in previous recipe.

Stuffed Roast Pheasant

1 large young pheasant, ½ lb. pork sausage meat, ¼ lb. chicken livers mashed, 1 truffle chopped, 1 tbs. chopped parsley, 1 egg, 2 tbs. cream, pepper and salt, 4 slices mild fat bacon.

FOR THE SAUCE

1 glass Madeira or sherry, 1 tbs. tomato purée, pinch nutmeg.

Mix the sausage meat, chicken liver, and parsley together with pepper and salt if needed. Bind with the egg and the cream and stuff the pheasant. Secure the bacon slices, cover with foil and roast in a moderate oven for 45 minutes. When the birds are about three quarters cooked, remove the foil. Add to the accumulated juices in the pan the Madeira, tomato purée and nutmeg. Return the pheasant to the oven and continue cooking without the foil for 15 minutes. Baste often with the sauce. Serve on croûtons of fried bread and pour the sauce over the pheasants : alternative stuffings may be made with chestnuts, breadcrumbs, mixed or not with the liver of the bird (see p. 40).

Pot Roast Pheasant

2 young pheasants, 4 very thin slices mild bacon, 3 oz. butter, salt and pepper, 1 small glass brandy, 1 cup rich stock.

Season the birds, tie on the fat and truss them. Take an earthenware dish just big enough to hold the pheasants. Put in the butter and the pheasants on top, cover with a tightly fitting lid or seal with foil. Cook in a medium oven (no. 4) for 1¼ hours. When the birds are tender flame them with the brandy; remove them on to a heated serving-dish. Add the stock to the cooking juices, stir well and keep hot. Serve the pheasants with a purée such as celery or those suitable for partridge. Hand the sauce separately.

Pot Roast of Pheasant with Cream

Cook as for pot roast (see above), but when three-quarters cooked, pour on 1¼ cups of cream. Baste with this often, and add a little lemon juice before serving.

Pheasant with Celery

1 pheasant, 4 thin slices fat bacon (2 diced), pepper, salt, 3 oz. butter, 1 glass Madeira or sherry, 1 cup stock, 2 coarsely cut heads of celery, 1 cup cream, 1 beaten egg yolk (optional).

Tie two slices of fat round the pheasant; while trussing it season well with pepper and salt. Brown and sauté in a heavy casserole with the diced bacon in 2 oz. butter for 15 minutes. Add a wine glass of Madeira or sherry and ½ cupful of stock. Braise for 1½–2 hours in oven (no. 3) on a very low heat. While the pheasant is cooking, simmer the chopped celery in the rest of the butter and 2 tablespoons of stock. When the pheasant is tender put it on a serving dish. Ten minutes before serving add the cream to the celery and mix it well with the cooking liquid. If it is too thin reduce this (on a moderate heat to prevent the cream separating), or thicken with the egg yolk. Pour the sauce over the pheasant. Serve with rice or noodles and a green salad.

Pheasant in Apples à la Normande

1 or 2 pheasants, salt, pepper, 2–4 lb. apples (not cooking apples), 6 oz. butter.

Slice the apples and brown lightly in 3 oz. butter. Heat the other half of the butter, and brown the seasoned pheasant gently on all sides. Take a fireproof dish just about large enough to take the pheasant and line it with a layer of the browned apples. Cover the birds entirely with the rest of the apples. Cook slowly in the oven on no. 4 for 1¼ hours if the pheasant is young; but about 2 hours for an older bird. Serve in the casserole.

Pheasant in Cream

1 or 2 small pheasants, 3–4 oz. butter, salt, pepper, wine-glass brandy, rich stock, game if possible, ½ pt cream.

Brown the trussed pheasant in a heavy pan in the butter, add salt and pepper. Finish cooking with the lid on the pan in a medium oven, basting often, for about 40 minutes. Take the pheasant out and keep it hot while the sauce is made. Add the brandy and stock and the cream to the pan juices, reduce by simmering for 5 minutes stirring all the time. Put the pheasant back, baste and cook for another 5 minutes. Serve with mashed potatoes or rice.

Pheasant roasted with grapes

1 or 2 pheasants, salt, pepper, 1 lb. white seedless grapes, 4 oz. butter, 1 cup stock (1 glass white wine).

Season the pheasant with salt and pepper inside and out. Put as many grapes inside the pheasant as will go in without squashing them. Sew up the opening. Pour the melted butter all over the birds and place them on their sides on a roasting rack. Warm the stock and pour it into the roasting pan – use this with the melted butter and grape juice to baste the birds every 10 minutes. Cook for about 45 minutes in a medium oven. When the pheasant is tender, keep it hot on a serving dish. Mix all the pan juices up with the crusty bits in the pan, bring to the boil and strain over the pheasants. Add a small glass of white wine to the pan juices if there is too little liquid for the sauce. Remove the thread from the pheasant. Serve with sauté potatoes, surrounding it with the grapes.

Pheasant with Sauerkraut

A pheasant plainly roasted or braised.

SAUERKRAUT

2 lb. sauerkraut, 2 oz. butter, 1 onion chopped, 10 crushed coriander seeds, 1 cup stock (chicken or veal), 1 glass white wine, salt and pepper, 1 liqueur glass Kirsch.

Wash and drain the sauerkraut. Melt the butter in a heavy pan and add the onion. When it bubbles add the sauerkraut and coriander. Stir with a wooden spoon while the sauerkraut gets hot, but do not let it burn. Pour in the white wine and 2 tablespoons stock. Continue cooking it very gently for about 45 minutes, adding the rest of the stock from time to time, so that the sauerkraut stays moist. Before serving, add pepper and salt as needed, and a liqueur glass of Kirsch for preference, or Polish Vodka. Place on a hot dish with the pheasant on top. Garnish with sausages or bacon.

Pheasant with Cabbage

See Partridge with Cabbage (p. 43).

Pheasant with Sour Cream

See Partridge with Sour Cream (p. 45).

Casseroled Pheasant

1 large pheasant, 1 tbs. olive oil, ¼ lb. diced bacon, 1 oz. flour.

FOR THE MARINADE

1 sliced onion, 2 sliced carrots, 2 crushed cloves garlic, 2 bay leaves, salt, black pepper, 4 juniper berries, 2 glasses red wine.

Cut the pheasant into enough serving pieces for four people, and marinate the pieces for two days. Drain and dry. Sauté the chopped bacon in the oil in a heavy casserole, add the pheasant and brown it. Sprinkle on the flour and pour on the strained marinade. Simmer gently on top of the stove with a closely fitting lid for 1½ hours. Remove pheasant, keep it hot on a dish. It there is too much fat, spoon it off, and if necessary, soak it off with kitchen paper. Bring the sauce to the boil, pour over the pheasant. Serve with a purée of potatoes.

Casserole of Pheasant with Pimentos

1 large pheasant, ¼ lb. streaky bacon in one piece, 1 sliced onion and carrot, 1 oz. pork fat or 2 tbs. oil, 1 clove garlic, bouquet garni, 2 sweet peppers, 4 small smoked sausages.

Brown the sliced onion and carrot and then the pheasant in the pork fat in a heavy pan. Add the piece of bacon, the garlic and bouquet garni, and enough stock and water to cover all the ingredients. Cover the pan and simmer gently for 1½ hours. About 20 minutes before serving add 4 small sausages (any of the fairly highly spiced variety, like the Greek or Spanish type), and the coarsely cut pimentos. Tinned pimentos should first be drained and added only about 10 minutes before serving. Take out the bacon, remove the skin and cut it up. Serve the pheasant surrounded by the sausages, bacon and pimentos, on rice. The pimentos can be cooked separately with tomatoes, and aubergines, in which case you will have a ratatouille to serve with the rice.

Grilled Pheasant

2 or 4 young pheasants, 4 oz. butter, salt and pepper, 1 cup very fine fresh breadcrumbs.

Split the pheasant down the back to lie flat. Melt the butter and coat the birds thickly with it. Cover with breadcrumbs, season with salt and pepper. Grill under a moderate heat about 10 minutes each side, turning twice during cooking and basting with the remains of the melted butter. Serve with a tart jelly (e.g. cranberry) and game chips, or alternatively with a sauce diable (see p. 168).

Pheasant à l'Orientale

Best for an older pheasant.

1 large pheasant, 2 oz. butter, 1 liqueur glass brandy, 1 cup blanched coarsely chopped almonds or walnuts, ¼ lb. seedless raisins, 1 glass orange juice, salt, pepper.

Brown the pheasant in the butter in a heavy pan and flame it with the brandy. Add the raisins, nuts and orange juice. The liquid should come about halfway up the pheasants; if there is not enough add a little white wine. Season with salt and pepper and simmer closely covered for 2 hours on top of the stove. If the sauce is too thin, thicken it with a knob of beurre manié. Serve with rice.

Salmis of Pheasant

See Salmis of Partridge (p. 49).

Terrine of Pheasant

See Terrine of Hare (pp. 127, 128).

Faisan à la Sainte Alliance

'Take a pheasant, hung until it is perfect to eat. Pluck it and inter-lard it carefully with the freshest and firmest pork fat you can find. Take two woodcocks. Bone and draw them and make two piles, one of the meat, the other of the entrails and livers. With the meat, make a stuffing by chopping it with steamed beef bone-marrow, a little grated pork fat, pepper, salt, fines herbes, and a quantity of good truffles, enough to stuff the pheasant completely. Take care to put in the stuffing in such a way that none falls out. This is some-times difficult when the bird is rather old. Nevertheless, there are various ways of achieving this end. One is to cut a slice of bread and tie it onto the bird with a string, so as to seal its breast. Cut a slice of bread which overlaps the laid-out pheasant from neck to tail by two inches. Next take the liver and entrails of the wood-cock. Pound in a mortar with two large truffles, an anchovy, a little grated pork fat and a piece of good fresh butter. Toast the bread and spread this paste evenly on it. Put this under the pheasant, prepared as indicated above, so that the bread will be thoroughly impregnated with the roasting juice. When the pheasant is cooked, serve it, elegantly couched on the slices of bread. Surround with Seville oranges and look forward with an easy mind to the out-come.'

From : Brillat-Savarin, *Physiologie du Goût.*

Pigeon

In Great Britain, the abundance and greed of the wood pigeon has exposed him to death all the year round. Farmers, especially in the corn-growing parts of the country, pick them off when they will since they are technically classed as vermin. However, because of their hearty appetites – they consume brussels sprouts as well as corn, beech nuts and acorns – and the variety of their diet, they make plump gamey birds. In France, they are bred especially for the table and often eaten at four weeks of age when they are known as pigeonneaux – squabs. They are consequently very tender, highly prized gastronomically, and expensive. The British pigeon is cheap, under-valued and sometimes tough. However, in 1970, twenty-five tons of pigeon were exported to France, where they sell for twice the price they fetch in England.

The young pigeon of whatever nationality has pinky-orange legs without scales, and is all plump breast. They are at their best from March to October and that is usually when they are seen in quantity in the shops.

If possible the pigeon should be hung for a day or two by the head so that the blood will drain away from the breast meat. Whatever their age, one pigeon is only enough for one person – the largest weigh $1\frac{1}{4}$ lb. Roasting and grilling should be reserved for only very young birds, but older birds can be casseroled and cooked slowly in innumerable delicious ways. They lend themselves easily to puddings and pies, partly because of their size and partly because they are so cheap.

All pigeons improve by being well larded and marinated which will improve their flavour and succulence. The average time for roasting a pigeon is about twenty minutes and for braising about an hour and a half.

Roast Pigeon with Parsley Butter

4 young pigeons, 4 oz. butter, 1 tbs. chopped parsley, salt, pepper, 4 thin slices pork fat, flour, 4 mushrooms (optional).

Chop parsley and mix evenly with 2 oz. of the butter, season with pepper and salt. Put a lump into each bird and tie on the fat. Place the birds breast down on a roasting rack. Cook for 20–25 minutes in a hot oven (no. 6–7), basting frequently with the rest of the butter. Five minutes before serving take off the bards and dredge the breasts with flour. Keep them breast-side up and brown.

As a change from the parsley butter stuffing add a little chopped sautéed mushroom. Serve with game chips and a green salad.

Stuffed Roast Pigeon

4 young pigeons, 4 slices white bread, 1 cup milk, 2 eggs, 2 tbs. currants, ½ tsp. ground nutmeg, 6 oz. butter, salt and pepper.

Steep crustless bread in milk until the milk is absorbed, meanwhile beat up the eggs. Squeeze out the surplus milk from the bread, and mix with the eggs, currants, nutmeg, salt and pepper and 2 oz. of butter. Mix the stuffing so that all the ingredients are evenly distributed. Stuff the pigeon, sew it up, then truss it. Roast for 20 minutes in oven (no. 6) until lightly brown; the frequent basting with the 4 oz. melted butter should keep the birds moist. For the last 5 minutes of cooking dredge the pigeons with flour and brown quickly. Serve with gooseberry or red-currant preserve and crisp salad of endive or chicory.

Spit Roast Pigeon

4 or more pigeons, 1 wine glass olive oil, ½ bottle red wine, 6 juniper berries, salt and pepper, herbs.

Clean the insides of the pigeons but put back the liver. Roast the pigeons on a barbecue fire or on an extemporized wood fire (grape-vines are good because the solid bits burn very slowly) for about 25 minutes, basting frequently with oil. When they are almost cooked pour half a bottle of red wine into the roasting pan with the juniper berries, salt and pepper and whatever herb you fancy and finish cooking the pigeons in this sauce. The most important thing about this recipe is to prevent the fire taking over from the cook.

It is easy to collect enough bits of old vine and slow burning pieces of wood in early autumn – if you happen to be in wine-growing country. If not, leave out the vines. If you do not have a spit, some large skewers will do if they are placed on a roasting rack over the fire.

Pot Roast Pigeon

4 preferably young pigeons, 4 oz. butter, 12 very small onions, ¼ lb. mushrooms, 4 rashers mild bacon diced, 1 liqueur glass brandy, 1 glass white wine, 1 cup meat stock, salt and pepper.

Brown the trussed pigeons in a sauteuse in the butter. Transfer them to an earthenware pot into which they fit quite tightly. Sauté briefly the onions and mushrooms in the same butter, with the diced bacon. Dilute the cooking juices with the brandy and wine, add the stock and bring to the boil. Season with pepper and salt and pour all the contents and mushrooms, onions and bacon over the pigeons. Make certain that the lid is tightly sealed – put a piece of foil between the pan and lid to make sure. Cook in oven (no. 3) for an hour. For older or larger pigeons allow an extra 20 minutes.

This is a pretty basic recipe for a slow method of cooking pigeon. The flavour can be varied by the addition of herbs, e.g. thyme, marjoram, one or two tomatoes, pimentos, and so on. The important thing is to keep the birds moist with fat, stock and preferably wine in a tightly covered pot.

Grilled Spatchcocked Pigeon

4 plump young pigeons, 6 oz. butter, pepper and salt, 4 slices bread.

Split the pigeons down the backbone so that they lie flat. Spread the butter evenly on the birds and sprinkle with freshly ground black pepper. Cook them gently under the grill for about 7 minutes either side, having placed the slices of bread under the grilling rack. Baste the pigeons frequently with the remains of the butter, melted. Season with salt and more pepper if necessary. Serve on the slices of bread which should have absorbed all the juices. A crisp green salad should be all that is necessary as an accompaniment.

Grilled Pigeon Tartare

A slightly different way of grilling pigeon is to dip them in fine white breadcrumbs after they have been covered with the melted butter. Baste them frequently with more melted butter. Serve with sauce tartare (see p. 173).

Transform pigeons of doubtful tenderness into succulent birds with the following recipe.

Braised Pigeon (See also Cold Braised Partridge, p. 49)

4 pigeons, 4 oz. butter, pepper and salt, 2 glasses white wine, 1 small glass brandy, juice of 1 lemon, 1 lb. Jerusalem artichokes, 4 pigeon livers.

Put 3 oz. butter in a heavy casserole, place the well-seasoned pigeons in it with 2 glasses white wine, and simmer for 1–1½ hours with the lid on. When they are tender, take them from the casserole, cut in half lengthwise and put them in a china or glass dish. Pour the brandy and lemon over them and leave for 1 hour, turning at least twice during that time. While the pigeons are marinating make a purée of Jerusalem artichokes, for which you will need 1 oz. butter. Sauté in the cooking juices the pigeon livers and mash them finely; add these to the brandy and lemon marinade and strain this mixture into the purée of artichokes; place the pigeons on top and reheat gently. The artichokes may be replaced by a purée of turnip, celery, boiled beans or peas. A spectacular cold dish but just as good to eat hot.

Pigeon with Cherries

4 pigeons, bouquet garni, salt, pepper, ½ lb. morello cherries, 1 liqueur glass Kirsch, ½ pt aspic jelly (see p. 165) if possible made with a calf's foot and pigeon stock.

Truss the pigeons, salt and pepper them and put them in a casserole with the bouquet garni and enough water to come half-way up the birds. Cook in a slow oven (no. 3) for 3 hours. Look inside the casserole occasionally and add more hot water if the liquid is evaporating too fast. While the pigeons are cooking, soak the stoned cherries in the Kirsch. (It is difficult to get fresh morello cherries in England but the jars of imported cherries from eastern European countries are good, cheap and very easy to stone. If using these, strain off the liquid.) When the pigeons are tender put them on a serving dish and cut in half. If they are to be eaten hot, heat the cherries and serve the pigeons surrounded by them. To serve cold, make some jelly with the pigeon stock (see p. 17). Let the jelly cool and pour it over the pigeons and cherries.

Stewed Pigeon with Lettuces

4 pigeons, preferably young but older ones will do, 4 chopped shallots, handful chopped parsley, 8 cos lettuces, 1 pt meat or poultry stock, 4 rashers of mild bacon, 1 egg yolk, lemon juice, pepper, salt.

Cook the pigeons in boiling water for 5 minutes and cut them in half lengthwise. Blanch the lettuces in boiling water for 2 minutes. Drain the lettuces, cut them in two, also lengthwise; sprinkle on them the shallots, parsley and seasoning. Lay each half pigeon on the lettuce, and tie them up. Line a shallow wide casserole with the bacon rashers and place the lettuce-encased pigeons on them. Pour in the stock and cook very slowly for 1¾ hours. Drain the pigeons and lettuce so that as little of the sauce is left on them as possible, and put them on a heated dish. Thicken the sauce with egg yolk, add a teaspoon of lemon juice and pour over the pigeons. Serve with rice.

In the summer when there are plenty of lettuces and pigeons this is an ideal way of using both.

Pigeon with Green Peas

4 pigeons, 4 slices of fat, 3 oz. butter, salt, pepper, 4 cups green peas, ½ pt stock.

Brown the pigeons, barded, in butter in a heavy stewpan. Add the pepper and salt and the stock. Cover the pan closely and cook gently for about 1 hour, or longer if the pigeons are old, then add the peas and cook for another ¾ hour, or until the pigeons are tender. Serve with pommes Anna or dauphines (see p. 163) if potatoes seem necessary.

Pigeon with Olives

4 youngish pigeons, 4 slices salt pork fat, 4 thin streaky bacon rashers, 2 chopped onions, 2 oz. butter, 1 glass white wine, salt, pepper, 1 pt stock, 1 tbs. potato flour, 2 cups stoned green olives.

Bard the pigeons and put them with the onions and bacon into a heavy pan with the butter. Season with salt and pepper and add the wine. Cover the pan and simmer gently for 40 minutes, until almost all the liquid has evaporated – the pigeons should be half cooked by now. Pour in half of the warmed stock and thicken the rest with the potato flour and add it to the pigeons. Cover the pan again and cook gently for another 40 minutes. Add the olives 10 minutes before serving. If the sauce seems too thin add a knob of beurre manié. (If the olives are too salt blanch them in boiling water for 3 minutes before adding to the pigeons.) Serve with purée of celeriac, potatoes or brown lentils followed by a green salad.

Casserole of Pigeons as in Provence

4 pigeons, 4 oz. diced bacon, 3 oz. butter, 2 glasses red or white wine, 1 pt stock, 1 chopped clove garlic, 12 stoned black olives, 12 button onions, 1 tbs. chopped parsley, bouquet garni, salt, pepper. Marinate old pigeons (for marinade, see p. 117).

If they are old pigeons marinate them for 8 hours. Brown the trussed birds in 2 oz. butter with the diced bacon in a very heavy pan. Add the red wine, stock, bouquet garni, salt, pepper and garlic; cover and simmer either on top of the stove or in the oven for 2 or 3 hours according to the age of the birds. Half an hour before serving, add the black olives and the button onions sautéed in a little butter. Serve with chopped parsley sprinkled on the birds and some ratatouille (see p. 164) and crisp French bread.

Try larding the breast of the pigeons with fillets of anchovies, two to each pigeon. Whether the anchovies are in oil or brine use little or no salt in the cooking. Two or three roughly chopped tomatoes combine very well with the flavour added by the anchovy fillets.

Casseroled Pigeon with Cabbage

See Casseroled Partridge (p. 47).

Casserole of Pigeon

4 pigeons, pepper, 4 oz. butter, 2 oz. cubed bacon, 4 glasses red wine, ½ pt stock, 1 tbs. flour.

Marinate old pigeons overnight; young ones can be cooked without marinating.

Brown the peppered pigeons in 2 oz. of the butter with the bacon in a heavy pan; add the stock, cover the pan and simmer for 1½–2 hours, depending on the age of the birds. Fifteen minutes before serving, add the red wine. Sauté the mushrooms briefly in butter and season. Add them to the casserole and simmer for 5 minutes. Put the pigeons, surrounded by the mushrooms, on to a dish. Strain the sauce and thicken with the brown roux (see p. 24) made from the remaining butter and flour.

Pigeons with Sour Cream

See Partridges with Sour Cream (p. 45).

Fricassée of Pigeons

4 young pigeons, 2 tsp. salt, 2 oz. melted butter, 4 glasses white wine, pepper, ½ lb. sliced sautéed mushrooms, 1 oz. flour, ½ pt stock, 1 tbs. chopped parsley, 1 cup cream, juice of ½ lemon (optional).

Split the pigeons down the back; put them in a dish, sprinkle each with ½ tsp. salt and let it stand for an hour. Brush the pigeons generously with melted butter, add the wine, season with pepper. Cover tightly and cook slowly for 1½ hours. Fifteen minutes before the pigeons are finished add the mushrooms. Put the tender birds and mushrooms on a dish and keep warm. Stir the flour gradually into the sauce, add the stock and parsley, and make a good thick sauce. Pour this over the pigeons, first adding the cream. Eat with freshly cooked mixed root vegetables and/or peas and beans.

If the cream seems too rich, add the juice of half a lemon to it before mixing with the sauce. Avoid boiling this, to prevent the cream separating.

A traditional English way of making pigeon pie – make more than just enough so that you can eat it cold as well – if there is any left.

Pigeon Pie (1)

6 young pigeons trussed, ¾ lb. thinly sliced tender beef raw, 2 tsp. chopped parsley, 1 tsp. salt and pepper, 1 cup veal stock, 1 lb. puff pastry, 6 hard-boiled eggs, greaseproof paper.

Take a shallow pie dish large enough to hold six very young pigeons. If the pie dish is too deep the stock will be insufficient to cook the birds. Lay the slice or slices of beef in the bottom of the dish so that the entire surface is covered. Arrange the trussed pigeons on top of the beef. Cut the hard-boiled eggs in two and arrange them between the pigeons. Add the salt and pepper and parsley to the veal stock and pour it into the pie dish. Roll out the pastry to just over ¼ inch thickness. Bake in an oven (no. 5) for 1 hour. Cover the pastry with greaseproof paper for the first 30 minutes. Take it off for the last 30 minutes' cooking. Serve with salad.

If there are plenty of pigeons it is nicer just to use the breasts – use the rest for soup or to make potted pigeon or for a pâté. Allow two pigeon breasts per portion.

Pigeon Pie (2)

4 young pigeons, 4 eggs, 4 oz. (approximately 1 tin) foie gras, or mild liver pâté, ½ lb. finely minced beef, ½ pt reduced meat stock, 1 small glass Madeira, port or sweet Vermouth, juice of ½ lemon, salt, pepper, ¾ lb. puff pastry.

Hard-boil the eggs, stuff each pigeon with a dessertspoonful of the foie gras and truss them. Spread a layer of the minced beef at the bottom of the pie dish. Arrange the pigeons on the minced beef, halve the eggs and arrange them between the pigeons. Pour the meat stock, wine, lemon juice with seasoning over the pigeons. Cover with the pastry and cook as in the previous recipe.

Pigeon Pudding

4 pigeons, ½ lb. diced beef, 4 hard-boiled eggs, salt, pepper, pinch ground allspice, 1 pt rich stock, 1 lb. suet pastry.

Cut the pigeons in half down the backbone, discard the legs and wings so that the pigeons fit neatly into the pudding basin. Line the pudding basin with the suet pastry. Put a layer of the beef at the bottom and then the pigeon breasts, the quartered eggs, and the rest of the beef evenly distributed. Pour the stock in, season with salt, pepper and allspice. Cover with a lid of the pastry and steam for 3½ hours. Serve with any green vegetable or follow with a salad. Use the legs and wings for pigeon soup (see p. 67).

Stuffed Pigeon Sauté

4 pigeons, 2 oz. butter, 1 tbs. olive oil, 2 oz. chopped ham, 1 oz. flour, 1 tbs. tomato purée, 1 cup chicken stock, 1 glass white wine, zest of 1 orange, 4 chopped cloves of garlic, bouquet garni, salt, pepper.

STUFFING

Chopped pigeons' livers, 4 oz. breadcrumbs, 2 oz. chopped bacon, 1 chopped shallot, 1 egg.

Mix together evenly all the ingredients for the stuffing. Divide equally between the pigeons and fill each bird with some. Truss the birds and sauté them in the oil and butter till they are well browned; place in a casserole just big enough to contain them. Cover them with the ham. Make a roux (see p. 24) with the fat remaining in the pan the pigeons were browned in, using 1 oz. flour. Stir in the tomato purée, wine and stock, season with salt and pepper, add the chopped garlic, boil up and add to the pigeons. Put in the bouquet and the orange peel. Cook in a moderate oven for 1 hour. Serve in the casserole with rice or potatoes.

Chaud-froid of Stuffed Pigeon

4 young pigeons, 1 sliced carrot and onion, 1 pt rich stock, bouquet garni, 1 small glass sherry, cooking foil.

STUFFING

1 rasher streaky bacon chopped, 1 cupful fresh breadcrumbs, 1 egg, pigeon livers, 1 shallot, 1 tbs. chopped parsley, pepper, salt.
½ pt Chaud-froid sauce, aspic jelly (see pp. 167, 165).

To make the stuffing, combine the finely chopped or minced liver and bacon with the other ingredients. Remove the spine and breast bones from the pigeons, sew them up before trussing and stuff them. Truss and tie securely each pigeon in a piece of muslin; place the birds in a pan on a bed of the vegetables and the pigeon bones. Add the stock, sherry, bouquet, salt and pepper, cover with foil and then the lid. Cook very slowly for 1½ hours at least. When they are quite tender let them cool, and cut them in half. Coat them with the chaud-froid sauce (see p. 167) and decorate according to your fancy. Spoon aspic jelly (see p. 165) over, and serve on a bed of lettuce.

Terrine of Pigeon

4 pigeons, 1 lb. belly of pork, 4 rashers of streaky bacon, 4 juniper berries, thyme or marjoram, liqueur glass of brandy, salt, pepper.

Cook in the same way as Terrine of Rabbit (see pp. 140, 141), for the same length of time.

A way of using the remainder of the pigeon when making pie or pudding, using only the breasts:

Pigeon Soup

Legs and wings of 4 pigeons, pepper, salt, sprig of thyme, 1 onion, chopped basil or tarragon to taste, 2 pts stock.

Simmer the pieces of pigeon in 2 pints of liquid – half milk and half stock – for 2 hours. Season with pepper, salt, thyme and one onion. When the pigeon is tender take off the flesh from the bones. Return it to the broth. Pour in a spoonful of either fresh or sour cream before serving. Sprinkle freshly chopped basil or a very little tarragon before serving with croûtons.

If a whole pigeon is used instead, before serving cut the breast meat into cubes. Freshly chopped cucumber also makes a delicious garnish.

Woodcock

The praises of the woodcock have been sung by gourmets in both verse and prose, but the following incident, which I witnessed, shows the esteem in which it is still held. The occasion was a cooking tournament where the famous French chef and restaurateur, Raymond Oliver, was one of the competitors. Having cooked the woodcock with astonishing speed and dispatched it with champagne nature, Monsieur Oliver released a basketful of white doves which he claimed were the ascending souls of the woodcock.

British woodcock are in season between 1 October and 31 January, but most delicious in November and December, when they are at their fattest. Happily for the gourmet they are omnivorous and will eat berries, shoots, insects and worms.

An average woodcock weighs about twelve ounces, and one is enough for an average appetite. Unlike many game birds, the breast is not the best part; these are the legs and entrails when roast, plus the wings when stewed or cooked in a salmis.

They are plucked all over including the head, which is left on; this is twisted round, and, using the long bill like a skewer, is tucked round the thigh into the body.

The section of the spine in the neck must be removed first. Woodcock is not drawn but the eyes are removed. Certain woodcock eaters disapprove of this way of trussing them on aesthetic and moral grounds that it demeans a fine-looking bird. They prefer them trussed in the usual way.

Roast Woodcock

4–8 woodcock, 4–8 slices of fat bacon and bread, 1 tsp. lemon juice, 1 tsp. brandy, salt, pepper.

Bard the woodcocks, and leave them undrawn. Roast them for 15–20 minutes in a hot oven.. When they are ready take out the entrails. Discard the gizzard but mash the rest with 1 teaspoon of lemon juice, a teaspoon of brandy, salt and pepper. Heat this briefly in small saucepan and spread it on the pieces of toast. Remove the fat slices and serve each woodcock on a piece of toast with lemon segments.

An alternative is to add an ounce of butter and a dessertspoonful of mashed foie gras to the entrails.

Pot Roast Woodcock

4–8 woodcock, 4–8 oz. butter, 4–8 rashers of bacon, pepper, salt, fresh thyme (if not fresh, ¼ tsp. very finely ground).

(Remove the entrails if any of the guests prefer not to eat them.) Tie a rasher of bacon round each bird. Put 2–3 oz. butter in an earthenware casserole just large enough to fit the birds. Cover with foil and then the lid. Cook in oven (no. 5) for 20–25 minutes. Make a slice of fried bread for each bird. Mash the entrails with an ounce of butter, salt, pepper and thyme. Spread this on the fried bread and heat them briefly in the oven.

Serve each woodcock on either a plain fried croûton, or, for those who like it, with the mashed entrails. Pour the pan juices over the woodcock before serving.

Roast Stuffed Woodcock

See Roast Woodcock (p. 68).

Draw the woodcock, discard the gizzard, mash the entrails and mix them with 2 oz. finely chopped bacon, a tablespoon of finely chopped parsley, pepper and salt. Stuff each woodcock with some of the mixture. Truss the birds, brush them thickly with butter and roast.

Garnish with watercress.

Woodcock Salmis

See Grouse Salmis (p. 35).

Quail

The quail is the most common game bird in the United States – in certain areas the names for partridge and quail are interchangeable. But in America, like Britain and France, they are mostly farm-bred now. Formerly the quail were trapped and fattened up for the market. Exhausted by their flight across the Mediterranean from tropical Africa, quail was an easy quarry for the trapper. Alternatively they were imported from Egypt, where they rested, it is said, on their migratory journey.

The flavour of the farm-bred quail is rather flat compared to the wild bird, much as the domesticated rabbit is to its wild counterpart.

No hanging is necessary for quail, for they should be eaten as soon as possible after they have been killed. One quail weighs from two to six ounces, so that at least one, and preferably two, should be allowed for a serving. They are best roast either on a spit or in the oven. For those who find their flavour too flat cooked this way, any way of cooking partridge en casserole is suitable for quail.

After the quail has been plucked and drawn from the neck, cut off the tips of the wings. Truss like pigeon.

Roast Quail (1)

8 quails, 8–16 vine leaves depending on their size, 8 slices mild fat bacon, 8 pieces toast, melted butter.

Wrap each quail in enough vine leaves (see p. 39) to cover it and then tie on the slices of bacon securely. Roast for 10–12 minutes in a hot oven or on a spit. Put the slices of toast under the rack so that they catch all the dripping. Serve on the toast and garnish with watercress and wedges of lemon.

Roast Quail (2)

Roast the quail as in the previous recipe but serve it with a sauce made as follows :
½ glass of port, ½ oz. butter, 1 tbs. foie gras.

Mix the port with all the pan juices. Spread the toast with foie gras and serve with a quail on each slice. Dry red wine or sherry or Madeira may be used instead of port.

Quail Orientale

4–8 quails, salt, pepper, 2 oz. butter.

STUFFING

½ cup cooked rice, ½ cup seedless raisins soaked in ½ glass red wine, grated rind of 1 orange, 2 oz. butter.

Mix the ingredients for the stuffing together with ½ oz. of the butter. Season the quail with salt and pepper and spread the remains of the butter generously over the birds. Cover the birds with foil for the first 10 minutes of cooking in a hot oven (no. 7). Take off the foil, turn down the oven and roast for another 20 minutes basting frequently with the butter, orange juice and wine. Adjust seasoning. Serve the quail and sauce separately, with endive and orange salad.

Grilled Quails

4 quails, 2 cupfuls white breadcrumbs, 4 oz. butter, 4 large mushrooms, 2 tsp. paprika, pepper and salt, 1 glass sherry or Madeira.

Melt half the butter; split the quails down the back and season with salt, pepper and paprika. Brush the quails both sides with melted butter, and dip them in the breadcrumbs. Grill slowly for about 10 minutes on each side. When they are nearly cooked, sauté the mushrooms. Add the sherry to the butter in which the mushrooms were cooked. Serve the quails with the mushrooms and sauce accompanied by potatoes, rice or on slices of fried bread.

Devilled Quails

Grill the quails as in the preceding recipe. Halfway through the cooking, make a thick sauce with 2 tablespoons of made mustard and ½ pt of cream. Season with salt and spread over the quails. Put them under the grill for 5 minutes and serve.

Quail Sautéed with Brandy

4–8 quails, ½ wine glass brandy, 4 oz. butter, salt, pepper, bouquet garni, 1 tbs. flour, 1 glass white wine, ½ cup stock.

Flame the quails with the brandy in a sauteuse on top of the stove. Add a bouquet garni, season with salt and pepper and sauté briskly in the butter on a moderate fire. Turn them over often during cooking. When the birds are nicely browned and tender, sprinkle the flour onto the fat in the pan and gradually add the wine and stock, making a smooth sauce. Put the quails on a heated serving dish, remove the bouquet and pour the sauce over them. Serve with a salad of endive or lettuce.

The following is for a gala occasion where cost is secondary and skill is important.

Quail with Truffles, Foie Gras and Champagne
4–8 quails

FOR THE STUFFING
4 oz. ham chopped, truffles (according to taste, but 4 will do), 1 oz. butter.

THE REST
8 oz. butter, 2 glasses of champagne, ½ cup chicken stock, 4–8 large mushrooms, 1 small tin or 4 oz. foie gras, 1 liqueur glass sherry.

Make a stuffing of the ham, truffles and 1 oz. butter. Stuff each quail with some of the mixture and truss them. Braise the quail in a heavy pan in the butter on a moderate fire for 30 minutes. Season with salt and pepper. Take the tender quail out and keep them hot in a serving dish. Pour the champagne and chicken stock into the pan juices, boil quickly for 3 minutes to reduce a little, then add the truffles. Keep the sauce hot while the mushroom caps are briefly sautéed in butter. Cover each mushroom with a little chopped foie gras, sprinkle with sherry and place them on a heated dish. Put the quails on top and pour the hot sauce over them and serve.

Quails with Cream

4–8 quails, 4–8 slices bacon, 8 chopped shallots, 2 oz. butter, 1 small glass brandy, salt, pepper, 1 cup cream, 1 tsp. grated horseradish.

Tie the bacon slices securely onto the quail and brown them with the shallots in a shallow heavy pan. Flame the quails with the brandy, season them with salt and pepper. Add the stock and finish cooking in a moderate oven for 20–30 minutes. Take the quails out, put them on a dish and keep them warm; add the cream and horseradish to the pan and heat on top of the stove. Pour the sauce over the quails. Serve on croûtons with a green salad.

Quails Casseroled with Grapes

4–8 quails, 4–8 vine leaves, 4–8 slices mild streaky bacon, 2 oz. butter, 1 tbs. olive oil, ½ wine glass brandy, pepper, 1 lb. seedless grapes.

Wrap vine leaves and bacon round the quails as in roast quail (see p. 70). Brown them in the mixed butter and oil for 10 minutes turning them over often. Season with pepper and put them with the grapes into a casserole. Cook them uncovered in a medium oven for 15 minutes. Meanwhile, add the brandy to the pan juices, in which the quails were browned, making a demi-glaze in this way. Pour the sauce over the birds. Serve surrounded by the grapes, with crisp French bread.

The flavour is even better if the vine leaves are soaked in a little brandy first. If they are the preserved type, blanch them first and strain them before soaking in the brandy. As an alternative to grapes, stuff the quails with morello cherries.

Stewed Quail

4 quails, 3 oz. pork fat, 1 tbs. flour, 1 cup veal stock, salt, pepper, bouquet garni, 6 mushrooms, 1 globe artichoke, juice of 1 orange.

Cut the quails in half, sprinkle with flour and heat the fat until it bubbles; sauté the quails in it for about 5 minutes in all. Add the stock, salt and pepper, the bouquet garni, the mushrooms and the cut-up artichoke. Cook very gently for 1 hour in a covered pan. Just before serving, add the orange juice. A purée of potatoes or rice goes well with this.

Plover

There are, in descending order of gastronomic merit, the golden, the grey, and the green plover; only the first two may now be shot, between 1 September and 31 January in Great Britain. They are plentiful in Norfolk but some say that the prohibition on taking plovers' eggs has reduced their numbers. Evidently when two eggs were taken from the plover's nest she promptly laid another two, so that the production of plover chicks was increased by an automatic natural instinct. Whether this is a story put about by those who feel deprived by the absence of plovers' eggs, I do not know, but that there are very few plovers to be seen in shops is certainly true.

Plover, like woodcock, and snipe, are cooked undrawn and preferably roasted in the oven or on a spit. Allow one plover per person.

Roast Plover

4 plovers, 4 slices toast, 4 oz. melted butter, salt, pepper.

Put the trussed, undrawn plovers on to the roasting rack with the toast underneath. Brush the plovers with melted butter seasoned with pepper and salt. Roast in a moderately hot oven (no. 5) for 25 minutes, basting frequently with melted butter. About 5 minutes before they are ready, dredge (see p. 19) the breasts of the plovers with flour and let them brown. Serve on toast which should have absorbed the juice. A Madeira sauce (see p. 17), or olive oil, lemon and cayenne pepper sauce may be served separately. Garnish with watercress.

Stuffed Roast Plover

4–8 plovers, 4–8 rashers of mild fat bacon, ½ lb. stoned olives, 4–8 slices bread, pepper, salt.

Stuff each plover with 4–6 olives, season, tie on a rasher of bacon, truss them and roast for 10 minutes, basted with butter, in a hot oven. Place the slices of bread underneath the roasting rack. When the plovers are ready put them on a serving dish and keep hot. Brown the bread under the grill and serve the plovers on it.

Plovers Sauté

4 plovers cleaned and trussed, 2 truffles sliced thinly, bay leaf, salt, pepper, 1 pt stock, 1 small glass sherry, 1 tbs. flour, juice of 1 lemon.

Brown the plovers in butter, add the truffles, bay leaf, salt and pepper. Cook for another 10 minutes gently. Sprinkle on the flour, pour on the stock and sherry. Simmer for 20 minutes. Put the birds on a hot dish and keep warm. Bring the gravy to the boil and add the lemon juice. Strain the sauce over the plovers and serve with fried bread.

Wild Duck

There are a number of varieties of wild duck, but those that are eaten most often in Great Britain are the mallard, widgeon, pintail and teal. In the USA the canvas back is perhaps the most common. In the UK the permitted time for shooting them is between 1 September and 31 January, but under certain tidal conditions the period is extended to 20 February.

There are differing opinions as to the gastronomic hierarchy of the various species but there is a slight balance of favour towards the widgeon. It tends to keep away from the sea and feeds on short, sweet grass. It is at its best in October and November.

The mallard, which in England is synonymous with wild duck, is at its best in November and December. The pintail, which is widely distributed throughout Britain and Western Europe, is thought to be inferior to widgeon. The teal, which is the one most commonly seen in shops, is very good eating and at its best just before Christmas.

Sometimes the fishy flavour of wild duck can be unpleasantly obtrusive, but this can be reduced in two ways. It can be marinated in a strongly flavoured liquid and rubbed hard, both inside and out, with half a lemon dipped in salt. A raw potato, and onion or apple, pushed inside the body during cooking will tend to absorb any unpleasant flavour. In general, slight undercooking makes the duck better flavoured and more tender.

Unlike the domesticated duck, the wild duck is lean and should be barded with slices of fat during roasting. The addition of red wine in basting improves the flavour, as does the flaming of the bird with gin, whisky or brandy. It must be cooked within twenty-four hours of shooting, unless it has been bled first, as it is very liable to produce poisonous bacteria.

To pluck a wild duck without too much frustrating effort, pour melted paraffin wax over it and let it harden. When the wax is quite hard it should be pulled off, taking the feathers and down with it. Wipe the bird inside and out with a damp clean cloth – do not wash it.

Braised Wild Duck

4 wild ducks, 2 lemons, salt, pepper, 4 small onions, 4 small potatoes, 4 sliced carrots, 2 sliced onions.

MARINADE

2 glasses red wine, 1 glass port, salt, pepper, 4 slices streaky bacon, 4 carrots, 3 onions, bouquet garni, 1 pt stock.

Marinate the ducks with onion and potato inside the birds for 12 hours. Rub the ducks with lemon, salt and pepper. Sauté them in the bacon fat with the sliced vegetables with the lid on the pan for 20 minutes. Add the marinade; there should be enough liquid to come half-way up the ducks. If it is insufficient, add some stock. Season with pepper, if necessary, and add the rest of the stock. Cover the pan again and cook for another 30 minutes. If the sauce needs thickening, do so with a little beurre manié (see p. 22). Remove any excessive fat just by skimming it off with a spoon and then with some kitchen paper. Cut the ducks in two. Serve with red cabbage and the sauce separately.

Wild Duck in Red Wine Sauce

2–4 wild ducks with their livers chopped, 2 oz. bacon finely chopped, 1 tbs. parsley, salt and pepper, 2–4 slices fat bacon, 2 oz. butter, 2–4 onions and potatoes.

SAUCE

3 oz. flour, 1 pt stock, 1 glass red wine.
The flavour will be somewhat better if the ducks are not bled (see p. 76) before cooking.

Allow 2–3 hours with the onion and potato inside the ducks before stuffing. Mix the bacon and parsley with salt and pepper and the ducks' livers and stuff the birds with this. Tie the bacon slices on over the breasts and roast in a medium oven (no. 4) for ½ an hour. Make a brown roux (see p. 24) with the flour and butter and add the stock and wine. Put the cooked ducks onto a serving dish and keep warm. Add the pan juices to the sauce, stirring well. Strain the sauce and serve separately with the duck, with game chips and watercress garnish.

Pot Roast Mallard

2 mallards, 2 potatoes and onions, 4 slices streaky bacon, 4 oz. butter, salt, pepper, 1 glass port, ¼ pt cream.

By soaking the duck in salt water, the blood is extracted and for those who otherwise find unbled mallard is too powerful the flavour is improved.

Dry the ducks after 4 hours' soaking in salt water and put an onion and potato inside each one. Tie on the bacon slices. Put 4 oz. butter into a heavy pan and cover with foil and the lid and cook in a hot oven (no. 7) for 15 minutes; lower the heat (no. 5) and cook for another 15 minutes. Take the onions and potatoes out of the duck, and discard them; remove the bacon slices. Add the port to the pan juices, stirring it in, and then slowly add the cream while heating gently. Strain the sauce over the duck. Serve with potatoes, rice or noodles and a tart jelly preserve.

Braised Mallard and Cherries

2–4 mallards depending on size, 2 lemons, salt, pepper, 4 potatoes, onions, 3 oz. butter, 1 tbs. flour, 1 glass sherry, ½ lb. stoned black cherries (the tinned or bottled imported black cherries from central Europe are ideal for this purpose – drain off the liquid and use it, if necessary, for thinning the sauce).

Dip the halves of lemon into some pepper and salt and rub the ducks inside and out with them and put in the onions and potatoes. Brown the birds slowly in butter in a large sauteuse or frying-pan. Then put the ducks into a heavy casserole. Stir one tablespoonful of flour into the fat in the pan, then add the sherry gradually. When the sauce is smooth and thick add the cherries to the casserole; pour the sauce over the duck. Season with pepper and salt, cover the pan tightly and simmer for 1 hour until the ducks are tender. Serve on a potato purée.

Roast Teal

4 teal, 4 slices pork fat, 2 oz. butter, pepper and salt, 1 small glass port or Madeira or sherry, juice of ½ orange.

Put a knob of seasoned butter inside each bird. Tie on the fat slices securely. Roast the birds in a hot oven (no. 7) for 20 minutes, turning them over once or twice during cooking and baste with a mixture of the wine and orange juice and the melted fat. Remove the fat slices and serve with fried bread, or potatoes and salad.

Salmis of Wild Duck (See Salmis of Partridge, p. 49).

For 4 wild ducks, make ½ pt of stock with the giblets. As they will be half cooked for the first part of the operation by roasting, rub them with lemon, pepper and salt, and fill them with onion and apple in the usual way beforehand.

Wild Duck Bigarade with Bitter Orange

2 young wild ducks, 4 oz. butter, wine glass of port, 1 cup stock preferably veal, 1 tbs. flour, 1 liqueur glass curaçao, 2 Seville oranges, 2 tbs. lemon juice, 1 tbs. caster sugar.

Roast ducks for about 35 minutes in a medium-hot oven in a shallow pan in the butter, basting them often. Remove and keep hot. Make a roux (see p. 24) with the flour and pan juices, add the port and stock, stir well and add the skinned ducks, cut up into 4 pieces each; cook for about 15 minutes in this sauce. Peel oranges, removing only the coloured outside layer of skin (zest) and cut into matchstick slivers, for the bigarade sauce, which can be started while the ducks are cooking. Melt the sugar in a small pan adding the curaçao when the sugar turns yellow. Pour in the sauce from the ducks and the cut-up orange skin and lemon juice, bring to the boil and, at the last moment, add the flesh of the 2 oranges cut into smallish pieces. Serve with the sauce poured over the ducks, and potatoes, either sauté or roast.

Wild Duck with Port

2 wild ducks, 2 slices fat bacon, 1 small glass each of claret and port, 1 tbs. flour, ¾ oz. butter, 2 tbs. brandy, ½ cupful stock.

Roast the barded ducks in a fairly hot oven for about 15 minutes, season and baste often. When about half cooked, i.e. when the birds can be carved with a sharp knife, they should be taken out of the oven. Carve fillets from the breasts and the meat from the thighs and place on a warmed fire-proof dish. Make a sauce with a roux (see p. 24) made from a nut of butter and the flour with the port and the claret, and reduce to about half. Flame the duck flesh with the brandy and continue to keep hot. Add the juices from the carved birds to the sauce and the remainder of the butter in very small pieces. Serve with sauce poured onto the duck and red cabbage.

Miscellaneous Game Birds

Snipe

Snipe has a marginally lower rating than woodcock, although the American snipe is said to have a very delicate flavour. In Britain snipe spends its first days on marshy grounds, where it feeds on worms and snails, and perhaps this accounts for its slightly fishy tasting flesh.

Although snipe is in season in Britain from 12 August to 31 January, it is at its best in the cold winter months. Despite its plumpness, snipe can weigh as little as two ounces and go up to ten ounces. Allow one or two per person, or more depending on the size of the bird. Snipe is rarely seen in the shops and is generally the prerogative of the sportsman and his friends.

The young snipe has thin flexible feet and a long, dry bill. Snipe is plucked and trussed like woodcock and also left undrawn. For those who detect a faint mustiness in snipe, skinning is the remedy. Since the skin is quite soft, it will pull off like a kid glove, if one starts to pull gently from the legs or neck. In this case, it is necessary to cut off the head first.

Any method of cooking woodcock is also suitable for snipe, but roasting is the favourite method.

Black Game

Black Game is in season from 20 August to 10 December, but the exact dates vary from one part of the country to the other. It is at its best in October.

Larger than grouse, this bird will serve three or four people. Hang for six to seven days. As the flesh is dry, bard it and roast for 45–60 minutes with a biggish nut of butter inside. Black game can be served in the same ways as grouse.

Capercaillie or Cailzie

Although a member of the grouse family, and the largest game bird in Great Britain, the capercaillie is considered very poor eating. Its turpentiney flavour may possibly be eliminated by very lengthy soaking in milk. It is in season at the same time as grouse, from 20 August to 10 December.

It is found in the highlands of Scotland and although an attempt was made to increase the breeding, they are still rare. Hang for six to seven days before roasting for 45–50 minutes.

Hazel Grouse or Gelinotte

These, I am told, are not imported into Britain any longer from Europe; however, they are quite common there. In France hazel grouse is available during the winter, and many are imported there from Russia.

Like the capercaillie, a way of eliminating the turpentiney flavour from these birds is to marinate them in milk before cooking. Recipes for partridges are suitable for hazel grouse.

Ortolan

Ortolans are very rarely seen in Britain but they are fairly plentiful in certain parts of France. They flourish in south-west France in the area known as Les Landes, a seemingly unending stretch of pine forests.

The ortolan is surely one of the compensations for having to live there, but its slightly turpentiney taste is not to everybody's liking. However, those that are trapped are fed on other grain and can be delicious. Two or three are necessary for a reasonable portion. They are best roasted but will respond well to any recipe for quail. Purists say that they should be roast only in their own fat but they are more commonly wrapped in vine leaves and a slice of bacon. The ortolan is not for those who think it barbaric to eat larks or thrushes.

Wild Goose and Turkey

These can be cooked in much the same way as the domesticated kind, with the difference that the meat of these wild birds is leaner and needs larding and slower cooking.

Wood Grouse or Coq de Bruyère

The largest feathered game in Europe – almost as big as a turkey. Common in northern Europe, rare in France, and not available in England. If you are lucky enough to come across one, use pheasant recipes.

Game Soups

Game Soup (1)

1 pigeon, grouse or partridge, 1 tbs. butter, 2 onions, 2–3 sticks celery, large bunch herbs, 6–8 peppercorns, 1 large glass red wine,

2 pts strong brown stock, 2 large mushrooms, 1 oz. butter, 1 oz. flour, 1 dessertspoon red-currant jelly, lemon juice, bouquet garni.

Brown bird in butter in a large pan, remove, add sliced vegetables (except mushrooms) and brown them slightly; put the bird back, add bouquet garni, peppercorns and wine. Cover and simmer for 1 hour or until the bird is tender. Remove the breast meat, return rest of bird and simmer without the lid for 20–30 minutes. Strain. Take 2 oz. butter, add sliced mushrooms, stir in flour and add the stock. Reboil, add jelly and simmer with the shredded breast meat or substitute carcass of cooked game if the breast meat is to be eaten separately.

Hare soup can be made in the same way, using bits that are not roasted. Instead of shredding, the meat from the game can be blended or pounded.

Game Soup (2)

Game carcasses, 1 onion, 1 clove garlic, 1 turnip, 2–3 carrots, herbs, peppercorns, mace, 3–4 pts brown stock, fresh white breadcrumbs, 2 egg yolks, 1 glass sherry, ½ gill cream (optional).

Put broken-up carcasses into a large pan, add the onion, garlic, and other vegetables cut up, the herbs and stock. Simmer for 2–3 hours, until the soup is strongly flavoured. Remove any meat from the bones, blend with half its weight in breadcrumbs soaked in the stock. Add to soup, season, and boil. Mix the sherry, beat the egg yolks with the cream and add to the soup. Serve with croûtons of fried bread.

Fin

Game Fish

Fishing is a far more widespread sport in Britain than hunting or shooting but the catch, unlike game birds and animals, seems to excite almost no attention as food. While it is reasonable to throw back into the water very immature fish, it seems unenterprising not to eat, or at least, to try out, the larger specimens.

The only fish which we would class as game, to be seen regularly in fishmongers in the United Kingdom, are salmon and trout. A few shops with a central European or Jewish clientele sell carp, bream, bass and pike. Carp is considered a great delicacy in Europe, and indeed in some countries is given the reverential treatment at Christmas that we accord to turkeys. In France the pike has produced a dish of international repute – the quenelles de brochet – which has given rise to as many eulogies as the pheasant.

In the United States, where there are so many different ethnic minorities, they are less conservative about eating freshwater fish; carp and pike are often seen in the shops. Predictably, good weather too makes it pleasanter for the sportsman to cook his catch by the banks of the river, and incidentally learn about cooking.

Perhaps now that the fight against the pollution of rivers in Britain is having some success, and the fish are breeding again in forgotten places, we can soon look forward to eating grayling, perch and tench again.

The signs of freshness in game fish are exactly the same as for any other kind of fish. They should have bright eyes, the gills should be red, the flesh firm, and the scales intact.

All fish should be gutted before cooking; eels are almost always skinned. When cleaning make sure that all the blood that sticks to the backbone is removed and get rid of the blackish membrane in the fish cavity by rubbing it with salt.

Average times for poaching are from 10–15 minutes per pound, the longer time for gelatinous fish, such as eel and carp. All methods of cooking other fish can be applied to game fish, and, strictly speaking, a matelote is fish stew made only with freshwater fish and red or white wine. Clarified butter should be used when frying fish à la meunière or when it is to be sautéed.

Allow at least half a pound of fish per person except perhaps for salmon and salmon trout, both of which are rich in fat and extremely filling. An average portion is 6 ounces, but for mousse recipes much less would be needed per portion.

If you do have to clean the fish yourself, lay it on a large sheet of paper, scrape off the scales with either a knife for this purpose or a scaler (see p. 28) starting from the tail and scraping towards the head. Cut through the skin of the belly and remove the entrails. To fillet a fish, lay it flat on a board or paper. Cut only as deeply as the bone from head to tail and remove the fillet on either side of the backbone. Turn the fish over and do the same for the other two fillets. With small fish which are to be filleted into two, only make a cut along the top side of the fish, i.e. opposite the belly and remove the fillets from the backbone.

Small fish can be cut into pieces quite easily with a strong kitchen knife or in some cases with kitchen scissors.

When stuffing fish, take care not to overfill it as the stuffing will probably swell and ooze out in cooking.

Garnishes for Fish

Chambord

This garnish, a very elaborate one, consists of small quenelles of fish, truffles sliced or cut to the size of marbles, tiny fried gudgeon, freshwater crayfish, cooked in court bouillon, and fried croûtons. In addition to this, a red wine sauce made with the fish stock is served. The chances of getting freshwater crayfish in English shops are very remote, but Dublin Bay prawns make a good substitute.

Matelote
(Not to be confused with stew)

A garnish composed of button onions, mushrooms and crayfish as well as croûtons. The last two ingredients may be omitted if the fish is served with a sauce.

Fish Jelly

This can be used as a basis for aspic. It is made with the trimmings, i.e. the head, bones, skin of fish (the more gelatinous the better) cooked in salted water or court bouillon. The liquid is reduced and allowed to set – the more the liquid is reduced the richer the jelly. Red wine is added to the fish stock to make the red wine jelly for cooking certain fish in.

1 lb. mixed trimmings of, preferably, whiting, turbot, or plaice, 4 quarts water, 2 onions sliced, ¼ lb. mushroom trimmings, a large bouquet garni (2 bay leaves, 4 sprigs thyme, 6 sprigs parsley), salt, pepper.

Simmer for 2 hours, reduce to at least one third the original quantity.

Stuffing for Fish

5 cups of breadcrumbs, ½ pt milk or water, 2 large finely chopped onions, 1 oz. butter, 2 chopped shallots, 2 tbs. white wine, 2 oz. mushrooms chopped, 1 tbs. parsley, 2 eggs, salt, pepper, grated nutmeg.

Press the liquid out of the chopped raw mushrooms. Pour the milk onto the breadcrumbs. Melt the onion in the butter and cook the shallots in the white wine until all the liquid has evaporated. Squeeze the milk out of the breadcrumbs and mix them thoroughly with the onions, shallots and mushrooms and parsley. Season the eggs with the salt, pepper and nutmeg and beat into the mixture.

Duxelles

A stuffing for fish made from chopped mushrooms, shallots, onions mixed with butter and oil, with all the moisture evaporated from the vegetables by sautéing.

Court Bouillon

This court bouillon is especially suitable for salmon, salmon trout, either whole or in large cuts. For a 2 lb. salmon a court bouillon of the following proportions is suitable.

7 pts water, 2 oz. sea salt, ¼ pt vinegar, 2 sliced carrots, 2 sliced onions, 6 sprigs parsley, 1 bay leaf, 1 sprig thyme, 2 tsp. crushed peppercorns. Use white wine instead of vinegar if the court bouillon is intended as an ingredient in a sauce.

Bring to the boil and simmer fairly briskly for 30 minutes. Strain and cool.

Bass

Bass are in season in Britain from 17 June to 13 March and they are often caught in estuarial waters before they make their way upriver. In America they are widely distributed and highly prized both for sport and eating. The bass has pinkish, lean, firm flesh and weighs from one to eight pounds.

Smaller fish are best fried, grilled or baked. It can also be cooked in many of the ways suitable for salmon. Large bass are usually poached and served with the conventional sauces (such as hollandaise) for poached fish.

The best way to clean bass is through the gills and a shallow cut in the belly. If the bass is to be poached, it should not be scaled. The skin can be more easily peeled off after cooking. Before frying, grilling or braising, scale the fish carefully as the skin is delicate.

Suitable for small fish or slices of larger fish.

Fried Bass

4 bass from 6–8 oz., 2 beaten eggs, pepper, salt, 2 cups breadcrumbs, parsley, lemons.

Dip the bass in the seasoned egg and breadcrumbs twice, allow it to stand for ½ hour so that the batter sets. Fry for 10 minutes in deep, smoking-hot fat. Drain and dry; garnish with sprigs of parsley and lemon quarters.

Braised Bass

A 2 lb. bass whole, pepper, salt, 1 tbs. chopped parsley, 4 oz. butter, 1 sliced carrot, 1 finely sliced onion, 1 bouquet garni, 2 glasses dry white wine.

For this method of cooking, scale the bass. Sauté the sliced onions and carrots for 5 minutes in ¼ oz. of butter. Season the bass with pepper and salt. Mix the parsley together with 1 oz. of the butter, season with pepper and salt and spread the paste over the inside of the fish. Cover the bottom of the saucepan with the sautéed vegetables and a bouquet garni. Pour the wine and 2 oz. of the butter, melted, over the fish. Cover the pan and bring to the boil on top of the stove. Then put it in a moderate oven, uncovered, and cook for 30 minutes basting it frequently. Drain the fish and place it on a dish. Reduce the braisage (the liquid it was cooked in) by one third and beat in 1 oz. melted butter and pour over the fish. Serve with boiled potatoes and the vegetables used in the cooking.

Braised Bass with Tomatoes

A 2–3 lb. bass scaled and cleaned, 1 oz. butter, 1 chopped onion, the flesh only of 6 skinned tomatoes coarsely chopped, 1 tbs. chopped parsley, a sprig of thyme, 1 bay leaf, ½ clove garlic crushed, 1 glass white wine.

SAUCE

1 oz. butter, flour.

Sauté the onions, tomatoes and garlic in a shallow pan or sauteuse with 1 oz. of butter, without browning them. Add the wine and bring to the boil. Put in the fish, cover the pan and cook in a moderate oven for 20 minutes. Drain the fish and keep hot in a dish. Strain the braising liquid and add 2 tablespoons of melted butter. Alternatively 2 tablespoons of velouté sauce (see p. 173) or a knob of beurre manié to make a thicker, smoother sauce.

Poached Bass

2 lb. bass whole, 3 pts court bouillon (see p. 23), parsley sprigs.

Put the bass into a warm court bouillon and bring it to the boil. Reduce the heat and simmer gently for 25 minutes. Drain the bass, dry and garnish with sprigs of parsley.

Serve with melted butter or hollandaise sauce (see p. 170) and boiled potatoes.

Poached bass is as good eaten cold as hot. It can then be served with mayonnaise or sauces suitable for cold fish (see p. 171) and salad.

Bream (Freshwater)

Bream weighs between one and three pounds, and is not nearly so good as carp. It can be cooked in the same way, but needs more seasoning to relieve the insipidity of flavour. They are mostly used in fish stews or matelotes.

Both bream and carp are usually sold whole, but it is as well to get the fishmonger to clean them. The scales, which are tough and numerous, are very difficult to get rid of in an ordinary kitchen; they bung up the sink and stick to every surface. Fishmongers have special gadgets, especially an outsize brush, which removes the scales in a flash. It is important to scrape out all the pieces of blood, which may adhere to the backbone, before cooking as this can taste rather bitter.

Carp

There are many varieties of carp, including the mirror, the leather, and the Bohemian carp: the family also includes the barbel, gudgeon, tench and bream, chub, roach, loach, dace, minnow and bleak. Only two – the carp and the bream – are eaten to any extent in Britain.

In the USA carp are particularly abundant in the rivers and lakes in the Middle West. There is also a large market for them, especially in the New York area.

The flesh is delicious, being fat and succulent; if it has any drawback, it is the quantity of small bones. Carp grow to a legendary age and can weigh as much as thirty pounds, but the average weight of those sold in shops is between two and seven pounds. Their habit of hibernating on the river bed in winter, when they eat very little, may account for their occasional muddy flavour. This can easily be cured by soaking the fish in two lots of slightly salted water with a spoonful of vinegar added.

Carp is in season from 17 June to 13 March in Britain, and at its best from November onwards.

Carp au Bleu

This is mainly for sportsmen as it is really only possible to cook fish 'au bleu' when they are freshly caught. Handle the fish as little as possible. Remove the gills and gut the fish quickly, cut off the fins etc. The 'bleu' depends on leaving as much of the natural slime on as possible. Sprinkle the fish with boiling hot vinegar and plunge into boiling court bouillon, if available, otherwise salted water. To cook, keep the water just hot enough so that it is perceptibly shivering. A small fish weighing from 5–8 ounces will be cooked in 15–25 minutes.

Serve with parsley garnish and skin just before serving. Fish 'au bleu' can be served hot with melted butter and boiled potatoes or cold with horseradish sauce (see p. 170).

Poached Carp

A 2 lb. carp, pepper, salt, 2 pts court bouillon (see p. 23).

Poach the carp in the court bouillon for 30 minutes on a low fire with the lid on the saucepan. Drain the fish. Garnish with sprigs of parsley. If it is to be served hot, accompany with melted butter or hollandaise sauce (see p. 170).

Fillets of Carp

4 fillets carp, pepper, salt, 2 pts court bouillon (see p. 23).

Season the carp and poach them gently in a shallow covered saucepan for 15 minutes. Drain and put them on a serving dish covered with any sauce suitable for poached fish (see p. 170).

This is a French way of stuffing a whole carp; the red wine used to cook it in and the stuffing are totally different from the central European Jewish way, but equally delicious.

Stuffed Carp (1)

A 2–3 lb. carp whole with roe, 3 pts court bouillon, pepper, salt, ½ glass burgundy, 16 button onions, ½ lb. mushrooms.

STUFFING

2 cups white breadcrumbs, 2 chopped shallots, carp roe, water, 1 tsp. fresh chopped tarragon, chives or parsley (or ½ tsp. dried), 2 oz. butter, 2 egg yolks.

Soak the breadcrumbs in water, sauté the shallots in ½ oz. of butter and pound the roe through a sieve. Squeeze the water out of the breadcrumbs, and mix the above ingredients together with the herbs and 2 oz. butter; bind the mixture with 2 egg yolks. Stuff the carp and sew up the opening. Season with pepper and salt, and pour ½ glass of burgundy over the fish. Poach it gently in the court bouillon for 30 minutes. When the carp is cooked, remove it from the fish kettle (or alternative pan). Add the burgundy, reduce the cooking liquid by two thirds and thicken it with beurre manié (see p. 22). Serve with a garnish of glazed button onions and mushrooms (see p. 162).

The stuffing in this case is made according to the Jewish recipes – not to be confused with the French recipe for Carp à la Juive !

Stuffed Carp (2)

A 3–4 lb. carp cleaned but left with the head on and the spine removed, 4 pts court bouillon (see p. 23), 2 sliced carrots.

STUFFING

1½ lb. filleted white fish – a mixture of haddock and hake or cod, 2 eggs, 2 finely chopped onions, 2 oz. butter, salt and pepper, 1 tbs. ground almonds, 1 cup fresh breadcrumbs or matzo meal,* 1 tbs. finely chopped parsley.

Pound the white fish or put it through the finest mincing blade, add the beaten eggs, salt, pepper, 1 tablespoon ground almonds, 1 cup fresh breadcrumbs or matzo meal. Melt the chopped onion in butter and add that to the other ingredients for the stuffing. Mix the parsley evenly through the mixture. Stuff the carp and sew it up. Poach the carp very slowly for 1½ hours in the court bouillon. Two thirds of the way through the cooking add 2 sliced carrots. When it is cooked remove the carp carefully and decorate it with the carrot.

To serve cold, reduce the bouillon by a quarter and let it set; serve diced on the carp. Thin slices of pickled cucumber can also be used for garnish. To serve hot, make an egg and lemon sauce with the fish stock (see p. 169). This dish serves 6 people.

A variation on this dish can be obtained by poaching the fish in

*Matzo meal is made from the unleavened bread originally eaten at Passover. Its advantage over flour is that although it can be as fine, it has already been cooked. It is ground in three sizes: coarse, medium and fine.

a mixture of half wine and rich fish stock and serving with sauer-kraut. It is then called Carpe à l'Alsacienne.

The following method of cooking carp is more suitable for small fish.

Fried Carp

4 or more small carp depending on size, 2 tbs. seasoned flour, 2 eggs, 1 cup milk.

Make a batter with the flour, eggs and milk, and allow it to stand for 30 minutes. Dip the carp in the batter. Heat the oil in a deep pan with a basket and when it gives off a blue haze put the carp in, one by one to prevent oil cooling. Fry for 7–10 minutes by which time the fish should be well browned and cooked inside. Drain and dry on absorbent paper. Serve with sauté or chipped potatoes and garnish with sprigs of parsley and quartered lemons.

Carp à la Provençale

A 2–3 lb. carp in 1-inch slices with the head, 1 pt water, 2 glasses red wine, 2 shallots, 2 cloves garlic, 2 oz. chopped mushrooms, 1 tbs. chopped parsley, salt, pepper.

Put the carp slices with the head into a casserole with 1 pint of warm water and 1 pint of red wine. Add shallots, garlic, mush-rooms, parsley, salt and pepper. Simmer slowly with the lid on for 30 minutes. Remove fish and keep hot. Reduce the sauce by half. Strain over the hot fish and serve. Boiled new potatoes are good with this.

Carp à la Juive

2½ lb. carp cut into 1-inch slices, 1 large chopped onion, 1 chopped shallot, 2 tbs. flour, 2 glasses white wine, 1 pt fish stock (or court bouillon), bouquet garni, salt, cayenne pepper.

Soften the onions and shallot in the oil without browning them, in a large saucepan. Add the flour and amalgamate it with the contents, cooking it for a minute. Add the white wine and fish stock and the bouquet garni. Season with salt and the cayenne pepper. Put the carp slices in with the head. Cook for 30 minutes on a low fire with the lid on. Take out the fish and arrange the slices on a dish to imitate its original shape, with the head. Reduce the strained stock by half and mix it, when it has cooled, with a small cup of olive oil, in much the same way as for a mayonnaise. Pour the sauce over the fish and allow the sauce to set. Sprinkle with chopped parsley.

Serve with horseradish and beetroot sauce (see p. 170). A variation on this method is to add 2 tablespoons of granulated sugar and 4 tablespoons of seedless raisins which have been soaked in a cup of water and 1 tablespoon of wine vinegar to the liquid after it has been mixed with the oil. By adding a pinch of saffron and 2 tablespoons of ground almonds to the oil mixture it becomes Carp à la Juive Orientale.

The Loire, besides having the best châteaux in France, also has some of the best freshwater fish – Chambord carp may well have appeared at a courtly table. Impressive for a dinner party.

Braised Carp à la Chambord

A 4 lb. carp, 4 strips bacon fat, 2–4 truffles sliced, 2 sliced carrots, 1 sliced onion, 2 sprigs parsley, 1 sprig dill, or pinch of dried dill, 2 oz. sautéed mushrooms, 1½ pts red wine fish stock, ½ cup fish glaze.

STUFFING

1 lb. fillet of sole or hake, ¼ lb. panada (see p. 23), 1 egg yolk, ½ cup cream, salt, pepper.
Chambord garnish (see p. 85), red wine sauce (see p. 174).

Make a stuffing in the same manner as for quenelles (see p. 101), omitting the white of egg and using sole or hake instead of freshwater fish. Stuff the fish and sew it up. Skin the fish round its middle, but not near the belly, otherwise the stuffing may ooze out. Cover the skinned part with 3 or 4 strips of bacon fat and/or slices of truffles. Cover the bottom of a fish kettle (or other saucepan) with the carrots, onion, parsley and dill as well as the sautéed mushrooms. Put the carp on top of the vegetables on a strainer or in muslin. Add the red wine and fish stock so that the fish is three-quarters covered by the liquid. Cover the saucepan and cook in a low oven (no. 2–3) for 45 minutes. Drain the carp and put it on a serving dish. Cover with glaze. Serve it surrounded with the Chambord garnish and red wine sauce made from the liquids in which the carp was braised.

Eel

The sharp-nosed English eel is the best of the species in Britain for eating, and it is at its peak from August to December. To augment the supply of eels, many are imported from Holland. They vary in weight from half to two pounds and can grow to two feet long. They must be kept alive until just before they are cooked. The usual way of killing them is to bang the head hard on a stone, or to cut off the head with a well-aimed sharp chopper. Skinning is tricky. Hang the eel by a string tied tight round the neck, make a light cut in the skin all round just below the string. Turn the skin down and hold it with a cloth and pull. With luck the skin will come off in one piece. Eels can be skinned more easily if they are grilled for a few moments under a fierce heat. Turn them over so that the skin blisters on all sides – it will come off easily then; this method also reduces the amount of fat in the eels. Cut down the belly and clean the inside part of the head.

In England the most usual way of cooking them is to boil and serve them jellied. For some strange reason the eel, which is not the most beautiful fish to look at, has remained popular in England, although mostly in urban working-class districts. It is equally delicious poached, stewed or made into pies, and is as good as, if not better than, salmon when it is smoked.

The first process for dishes of sautéed, fried or grilled eels may be preceded by simmering in court bouillon for 15 minutes.

Jellied Eels

2½ lb. cleaned eels cut into chunks, 1½ pts white wine court bouillon (see p. 23), ½ lb. mixed fish trimmings.

Marinate the chunks of eel overnight in the court bouillon. Reduce by poaching for 1 hour ½ lb. of fish bones, head and trimmings in 2 pints of water to make a jelly. Cook the eels in the marinade and melted jelly for 1¼ hours. Take out the eel, skin and bone the pieces and put them into a deep dish. Reduce the eel stock, simmering for 15 minutes, and skim off all the fat. Pour the strained liquid over the eels and allow to set. Serve cold.

This way of presenting jellied eels makes a splendid picture which deserves a large audience.

Galantine of Eel

4 lb. eel cut in chunks, 4 tbs. fresh chopped parsley, 3 pts fish jelly (see p. 85).

MARINADE

1 liqueur glass each of brandy and white port, juice of 1 lemon, 2 chopped carrots, 1 chopped onion, 1 crushed clove of garlic, 3 sprigs parsley, 2 bay leaves, 2 sprigs of thyme.

Marinate the eel for 1 hour, turning the pieces about every 15 minutes. Add the marinade to the jelly and poach the eels gently in this mixture for 1 hour. Drain the fish, take out the bones. Strain the fish stock and reduce it by about a quarter. Remove any fat from the liquid. Pour the reduced jelly into a wetted dish before putting the ingredients into it, arranged in alternate layers of fish and parsley, and let it set in the refrigerator or in a cool larder. Turn out the jelly when serving onto a dish of green salad. If you have a fish mould, so much the prettier.

Poached Eel

2 lb. skinned eel, 1½ pts court bouillon, 2 tbs. chopped parsley, salt, pepper.

Clean the eel and cut it into 1-inch wide chunks. Simmer in the court bouillon uncovered for 20 minutes and remove all the scum. Adjust the seasoning. Serve hot with a generous sprinkling of parsley and boiled potatoes, or cold with potato salad.

Eel Meunière

2 lb. fillet of eel, 2 oz. flour, salt, pepper, 4 oz. butter, 2 lemons quartered, 2 tbs. chopped parsley.

Dip the eel in the seasoned flour and sauté for 15 minutes in butter (clarified butter is much less likely to burn the fish). Turn them once or twice during cooking if you are not actually shaking the pan a good deal. Serve hot with a generous sprinkling of parsley. Sauté potatoes or lyonnaise (see p. 164) and a green salad go well with this dish.

Fried Eel

2 lb. fillet of eel, 2 cups fine breadcrumbs, 2 eggs, pepper, salt, tomato sauce (see p. 173).

Dip the fillets in breadcrumbs and seasoned beaten eggs, and fry in smoking-hot deep fat. Dry off surplus fat on kitchen paper and serve with tomato sauce. A thick batter (see p. 22) of flour, milk and eggs may be used instead of egg and breadcrumbs.

Grilled Eel

2 lb. eel, salt, pepper, 2 tbs. olive oil.

Score the eel and cut it up into 3-inch pieces, brush them with olive oil, season with salt and a generous sprinkling of black pepper. Grill for 7 minutes either side under a moderate heat. Serve with a maître d'hôtel butter (see p. 171) and mashed or sauté potatoes.

Grilled Eel with Red Wine Sauce

2 lb. eel, salt, pepper, 2 tbs. olive oil.

SAUCE

1 large glass red wine, 2 small chopped shallots, ½ oz. butter, 1 tbs. flour, pepper and salt, 1 tsp. chopped parsley.

Grill the eel as in the previous recipe. To make the wine sauce, put the shallots with the red wine and seasoning into a small saucepan and reduce the liquid to half. Thicken with a knob of beurre manié (see p. 22) and add the parsley. Serve with small new potatoes or as in the previous recipe.

Eels à la Provençale

2–3 lb. cleaned eel, salt, pepper, 2 oz. flour, 3 oz. butter, 2 tbs. olive oil, 1 cup breadcrumbs, 2 tbs. chopped parsley, 2 finely chopped cloves garlic, pinch dried thyme or tsp. fresh chopped.

Season the eel with salt and pepper. Chop into ½-inch slices. Roll them in flour and brown lightly in the bubbling mixture of butter and olive oil. Cook for about 15 minutes shaking the pan occasionally to prevent the fish sticking to it. When the eel is tender, sprinkle in the parsley, breadcrumbs, garlic and a little thyme, and more seasoning if necessary. Put the dish under a hot grill to brown the breadcrumbs quickly. Serve with a crisp green salad.

Eel Stewed in Red Wine

2½ lb. eel cut up into chunks, 1 finely chopped onion, 1 glass red wine, pepper, salt, bouquet garni, 2 oz. chopped mushroom stalks, 16 glazed button onions, ¼ lb. sautéed mushrooms, knob of beurre manié (see p. 22).

Sauté the eel and onion in the butter for 5 minutes, add the wine, onions, mushroom stalks and bouquet garni and simmer on a moderate heat for 15 minutes. Remove the eel chunks and put them in a shallow fire-proof dish. Thicken the cooking liquid with the beurre manié. Cover the eel, surrounded by the sautéed mushrooms and onions and simmer for 5 minutes. Garnish with prawns and little croûtons.

This dish can also be made with white wine, or vermouth, with 2 tablespoons of cream added to the sauce before serving.

Stewed Eel with Peas

2–3 lb. cleaned sliced eel, 4 oz. butter, 1 chopped onion, salt, pepper, 1 glass white wine, 1 lettuce, 1 lb. shelled green peas.

Sauté the eel in the butter in a casserole; add the onions, seasoning and white wine and simmer gently with a lid on for 15 minutes. Take out the eel and put half the lettuce at the bottom of the pot, then the peas and the pieces of eel on top. Cover with the other half of lettuce and cook for another 20 minutes. Serve hot from the casserole.

In the rice-growing areas of Valencia near the sea, eels are found in great numbers. Eel stews are made with a variety of ingredients. In this dish the rich red sauce made with the paprika (called pimenton in Spain) and oil is delicious – but not for stomachs unaccustomed to lavish use of olive oil. This is often served by beach restaurants, at least, those that haven't succumbed to what they think the tourists want.

Stewed Eels Valenciana

2 lb. eel cut in chunks, 2 cloves garlic, 12 nuts (hazel preferably but almonds will do), 1 tbs. paprika (pimenton), ½ cup olive oil, 2 tbs. flour, 1 tbs. chopped parsley, 4 black peppercorns, 1 glass white wine, salt.

Make a paste by pounding the garlic, nuts, paprika and peppercorns together in a mortar, and adding a tablespoon of water. Brown the flour in the olive oil in a saucepan, add the paste and a glass of white wine. Cook the eels in this sauce on a moderate heat for 20 minutes. Add salt and serve. A green salad is all that is needed, but crisp bread or boiled potatoes to mop up the sauce are nice.

Coiled Eel à la Carême

1 large whole eel boned, ½ lb. sole fillets, 1 beaten egg, ½ tsp. chopped tarragon, 2 pts (or more) court bouillon, 4 truffles sliced, 2 hard-boiled eggs, salt and pepper. The court bouillon should contain at least 2 glasses of white wine.

Mix the egg with the pounded sole, add salt and pepper. Stuff the eel with this mixture and sew it up. Twist the eel into a coil, keeping it in shape with string. (If you have a wire basket for deep frying to put the eel in before cooking, there will be no problem when removing it from the stock.) Place the eel in a deep saucepan and pour the court bouillon (see p. 23) over it so that it is completely covered. Poach very gently for 1¼ hours. Drain and let it cool, decorate it with sliced truffles and slices of hard-boiled eggs, and mask with a chaud-froid sauce (see p. 167). Serve on a bed of rice.

Pike

Pike are in season from August to March and, like the carp, are reputed to live to great ages. For culinary purposes, the best size for a pike is from two to four pounds. If a pike is hung from eight to twelve hours by the jaw, having had as much salt as possible thrust down its gullet, its flesh will be very tender. Also it has the effect of dissolving to some extent the small bones during cooking.

The white flesh of the pike is good baked, grilled, fried or poached, but its supreme dish is as quenelles. These are, roughly translated, a kind of dumpling, but of such exquisite lightness as to totally belie any connection with the heaviness evoked by that word.

Braised Pike with Mushrooms

1 pike about 3 lb., salt, pepper, 1 lb. mushrooms, 1 cup rich fish stock, ½ cup cream, 1 tsp. brandy.

Put the pike either on a strainer or in a muslin cloth in a fish kettle large enough to be able to lift the complete fish out of the saucepan. Surround the pike with mushrooms, add a cup of the rich fish stock, season and braise in a moderate oven with the lid on for 30 minutes. Put the fish on a serving dish. Reduce the sauce, add the cream and a teaspoon of brandy. Pour the sauce over the pike and serve.

Pike au Beurre Blanc

A 2 lb. pike, 1½ pts court bouillon (see p. 23), salt, pepper, 6–8 oz. butter for beurre blanc.

Clean the pike and lay it in a warm court bouillon in a shallow pan (or fish kettle); bring to the boil. Turn down the heat and poach very gently for 30 minutes. Remove the pike onto a heated dish and keep warm. Reduce the court bouillon to 2 tablespoons and make the beurre blanc (see p. 166). Pour over the pike and serve.

Pike with Anchovy

One 2 lb. pike, 8 anchovy fillets, 3 oz. butter, maître d'hôtel butter.

Clean and skin the pike and cut it into fillets. Lard the fillets with 2 anchovies for each fillet. Season with pepper (the anchovies will supply the salt), wrap it in buttered foil and bake it in a moderate oven for 20 minutes. Serve with maître d'hôtel butter (see p. 171) and new potatoes boiled.

Fillets of Pike

Fillets of a 2 lb. pike, 2 oz. butter, salt, pepper, 1 cup stock or white wine, cooking foil.

Lay the seasoned pike fillets in a buttered fire-proof dish with the stock or wine and baste them occasionally. If cooked in the oven, cover with foil to stop the fish getting too dry. Serve with a sauce gribiche (see p. 170) or any other preferred garnish (see p. 85).

Vary the flavour in cooking by laying the pike fillets on a bed of chopped, raw mushrooms, shallots and parsley. Make a sauce with the cooking liquid, add some hollandaise sauce (see p. 170) and brown it in a hot oven.

Stuffed Pike

See Stuffed Carp (p. 90).
The pike, like carp, can be stuffed whole or in cutlets.

Pike au Bleu

See Carp (p. 89).

Poached Pike

See Poached Carp (p. 90).

For a main course, and well worth the effort, are these almost lighter-than-air quenelles.

Quenelles of Pike

1 lb. cleaned and boned pike flesh, 2 oz. butter, salt, white pepper, 1 cup thick cream.

PANADA

4 eggs, yolk and white separated, 3 oz. flour, 1 oz. butter, 1 pt milk, pinch of nutmeg.

Pound the pike flesh from which all the bones have been removed with 2 oz. melted butter, salt and white pepper. Mix it with prepared frangipane panada (see p. 23). Let it stand on ice or in the refrigerator for 5 minutes. Beat the egg whites and add them to the mixture of pike and panada gradually, seasoning with more salt and pepper if necessary and a pinch of nutmeg. Chill this mixture in the refrigerator for 1 hour, or stand it on ice. Mix 8 tablespoons thick cream into the mixture. Mould the quenelles into 2-inch-long sausage shapes on a floured pastry-board, or shape with 2 spoons. Poach them in a fish stock or in enough salted water to cover the fish, in a shallow saucepan. If the pan is smeared with butter it prevents the quenelles sticking. Allow enough space for the quenelles to swell during cooking. Cook on a very low heat so that the liquid just trembles. Remove them carefully and drain on a cloth. Serve with a sauce nantua or mornay (see p. 171).

Quenelles may also be made with salmon or trout and other fish.

Quenelles of Pike Lyonnaises

Quenelles of pike are usually served with a rich sauce and cooked in salt water. For a change, they can be cooked in a brown sauce (see p. 166) flavoured with stoned olives, mushrooms, and other garnishes.

These are smoother and richer than the quenelles because of the additional cream.

Quenelles of Pike Mousseline

2 lb. pike boned and skinned, 4 whites of egg, 2 pts cream, 2 tsp. salt, ½ tsp. white pepper, pinch grated nutmeg.

Make the quenelles as before but with 2 pints of cream and cook in salted water.

Quenelles with Spinach

Make the quenelles as in either of the previous two recipes, then place them on a bed of puréed spinach seasoned with salt, pepper and a pinch of nutmeg. Pour the required quantity of mornay sauce (see p. 17) over the quenelles, sprinkle with grated parmesan cheese and brown quickly in a hot oven.

Trout

There are two kinds of freshwater trout – the rainbow trout and the brown trout. The latter are in season from March until September, the rainbow trout are available all the year round. Indeed, in certain restaurants they are kept in a tank and can be chosen by the customer. A trout fresh from the river or lake is delicious but shop-bought trout is so negative in flavour as to make its high prices an adequate deterrent. One trout per person makes just about enough for a portion. The most usual ways of cooking are grilled, sautéed, à la meunière (dipped in flour), or poached.

Grilled Trout

4 whole cleaned trout, pepper, salt, flour, 4 oz. butter, chopped parsley, lemon for maître d'hôtel butter.

Make 2 or 3 shallow cuts on both sides of the fish. Season with salt and pepper, dredge lightly with flour and brush with melted butter. Grill on a low heat for 7 minutes each side. Serve with maître d'hôtel butter (see p. 171) or other suitable sauces.

Fried Trout

4 river trout, 2 cups fine breadcrumbs, 2 beaten eggs, salt, pepper.

Dip the cleaned trout in the egg and then the breadcrumbs, twice. Let it stand, seasoned, for ½ hour while the coating tightens up. When the oil or fat in the deep-frying pan is smoking hot, fry the trout. When they are crisp and brown, drain and dry off all fat. Serve with colbert butter (see p. 168) and garnish with fried parsley.

Trout *Meunière*

4 whole trout cleaned, salt, pepper, flour, 4 oz. clarified butter, juice of 1 lemon, 4 tbs. cream, chopped parsley.

Season and flour the trout. Sauté quickly in the butter, turning twice during cooking. Before serving, add the lemon juice and cream to the butter in the pan. Serve on a heated dish and pour the warm sauce over the trout.

Alternatively, serve with chopped parsley and quartered lemons. Instead of chopped parsley and lemon, fry some finely chopped mushrooms and 2 teaspoons of breadcrumbs in 1 oz. butter in the same pan as the trout were cooked. When the butter is still foaming, pour over the fish. Add 6 capers and a squeeze of lemon to finish it off. A delicious garnish for trout is diced cucumber blanched and cooked in butter.

Trout *au Bleu*

See Carp au Bleu (p. 89).

Trout, like other freshwater fish cooked in this way, may be served hot or cold. Hollandaise sauce (see p. 170) is good with hot trout. Serve it cold with horseradish sauce (see p. 170).

Poached Trout *Chablis*

4 whole trout, ½ pt chablis or dry white wine, 2 sprigs fresh tarragon, 2 hard-boiled eggs, 1 pt white wine fish jelly (see p. 85).

Poach the trout in the white wine for 30 minutes. Put them on a dish, and allow to cool. Decorate them with the tarragon leaves and slices of hard-boiled egg and cover with the jelly diced.

This dish is equally good cooked with a dry red wine instead of the chablis.

Trout *en Papillotes*

4 trout filleted, salt and pepper, 3 oz. butter, 4 oz. duxelles (see p. 86), ½ cup velouté sauce (see p. 173).

Sauté the seasoned fillets in 3 oz. of butter so that they are half cooked. Lay each fillet on either half of the buttered paper. Mix the duxelles with the velouté sauce and put a layer on each of the 4 fillets. Cover the duxelles with the other fillet. Fold the papillotes and secure the edges. Cook in a hot oven for 10 minutes. Serve with sauté potatoes.

Stuffed Trout with Soft Roes

4 whole cleaned trout with roes (in this case, clean them after they have been boned as it is necessary to keep the belly intact), 1 glass white wine or fish stock, 2 oz. butter, ¼ pt cream.

STUFFING

2 finely chopped shallots, 2 oz. chopped mushrooms, 1 tbs. chopped parsley and chervil (fresh preferably), 1 beaten egg, salt, pepper, roes from the trout.

Mash the roes and mix them with the other ingredients for the stuffing. Slit the trout down the back from top to tail and take out the backbone. Lay some stuffing inside each fish and wrap each one in buttered foil. Put a glass of white wine or fish stock in the bottom of a dish and braise the fish for 20 minutes. Unwrap them and serve with a cream sauce (see p. 168).

Stuffed Trout Baked

4 ½-lb. trout, 3 oz. fish forcemeat (see p. 91), 3 oz. duxelles (see p. 86), 4 oz. butter (2 oz. for the sauce), 1 large finely chopped onion, ½ pt chablis, salt, pepper, flour, bouquet garni, anchovy essence.

Stuff the trout with a mixture of the forcemeat and duxelles, sew up the opening. Butter the baking dish, sprinkle the chopped onion on the bottom and lay the trout on the onion with a bouquet garni in the middle. Pour a tumbler (½ pt) chablis over the fish and dot with butter. Season and cook in a moderate oven for 30 minutes, basting often. Drain the trout, remove the thread and put them on a serving dish. Strain the cooking liquid through a fine strainer and heat it fiercely for ¼ minute. Add a knob of beurre manié to thicken it and then 2 oz. of butter and 3 or 4 drops of anchovy essence. Cover the trout and put it back in the very hottest oven for 1 minute to glaze.

Trout au Gratin

4 cleaned trout, salt, pepper, juice of 1 lemon, 2 tbs. water, 1 tbs. each chopped chives and parsley, ½ pt double cream, 1 cup breadcrumbs.

Spread butter generously on a baking dish just large enough to accommodate the trout. Season them with salt and pepper. Add the lemon juice and the water, sprinkle with the chives and parsley. Cook trout in a hot oven for 10 minutes. Meanwhile, boil ½ pt of double cream. When the fish are ready, pour the cream over them and sprinkle with breadcrumbs. Brown in oven and serve.

Miscellaneous Game Fish

Grayling

Grayling, unlike the trout to which it is related, is at its best in November. Small grayling, which weigh about 12 ounces, make the best eating. Like the perch, it is never seen in shops in Britain but highly prized in Europe. It can be cooked in any of the ways for trout, which is thought by some to be inferior in flavour to the grayling.

Smelts

Smelts, which are a very delicate small fish both in colour and flavour, are in season from September to May. To clean them it is only necessary to pull off the gills and the entrails will come out with them. Dry them gently but do not wash. They are usually fried and served very hot with fried parsley.

Perch

The perch is one of the most beautifully marked freshwater fishes of Europe, and it inhabits both lakes and rivers. A freshly caught perch is magnificent eating but the angler is in the best position to cook it in the most satisfactory way. This is to spear it on a sharp stick and grill it over a wood fire. A two-pound perch would be considered a fine large catch.

Perch is never seen in shops in Britain and even under-valued by the angler, but in Central Europe they are great delicacies. The American perch is known as the Yellow Perch.

Perch can be cooked in the same ways as grayling.

Salmon

In certain parts of north-east Scotland near the River Tay the salmon is known simply as the 'fish', whereas all other fish are known by the name of the species. It would be difficult to find a better way of showing the esteem in which the salmon is held there. But even if we don't all subscribe to this apotheosis, it seems to be generally agreed that salmon is the king of fish – not only of sea but of the river.

Salmon exist everywhere but the chilled salmon which is imported from Japan, Canada or Norway is a poor second in flavour to those from Scotland.

Although the height of the salmon season is in July and August, the flavour of those caught during the first two weeks of February in the River Tay is of a delicacy which vanishes later in the year.

A good fresh salmon will be stiff, shiny and have bright red gills. The medium-sized hen salmon is thought to be best – it can be recognized by its small head and thick neck.

To clean salmon, scale it gently, scrape away the blood after it has been gutted, and avoid too much washing.

Salmon may be poached, grilled or braised. It can be used in a mousse, soufflé or in the shell as in coquille St Jacques with a sauce. It is equally good hot or cold, smoked, potted and pickled.

For the very best salmon in its prime, use only slightly salted water to cook it in to preserve its delicate flavour.

Poached Salmon

4 salmon steaks, or 2 lb.-cut of salmon, 3 pts court bouillon or salted water.

Place the salmon in the cool court bouillon which should cover the fish. Bring it to the boil, reduce the heat and poach very gently for 15–20 minutes. Drain and dry it and serve with boiled or steamed potatoes. Sauces which go well with poached salmon are hollandaise (see p. 170), or béarnaise (see p. 165), plain melted butter, anchovy or maître d'hôtel butter (see p. 171).

Braised Salmon in White Wine

4 salmon steaks, 2 sliced carrots, 1 finely sliced onion, bouquet garni, salt, pepper, 4 oz. butter, 3 glasses white wine, ½ oz. butter and ½ oz. flour for beurre manié.

Butter a fire-proof baking dish, lay the vegetables on top with the bouquet garni, salt and pepper, and sauté them for 10 minutes. Lay the fish on top of the vegetables and pour the rest of the melted butter and wine over the fish. Cover the dish with foil and cook in a moderate oven for ½ hour, basting it from time to time. Take out the fish and put it on a heated dish, keeping it warm. Strain the liquid into a saucepan, reduce it by one third and add a knob of beurre manié to thicken it. Serve with the usual accompaniments.

Grilled Salmon

4 slices salmon, salt, pepper, 2 oz. melted butter.

Butter a fire-proof dish, heat the grill. Season the fish all over with salt and pepper. Pour half the remaining butter melted over the fish and cook under the grill, not too close to the heat, for 5 minutes. Turn the fish over, cover with the rest of the melted butter and cook the other side. Serve with maître d'hôtel butter (see p. 17).

Braised Salmon

A 2 lb. cut of salmon, 3 oz. butter, pepper, salt, 3 sliced carrots, 2 sliced onions, bouquet garni, 1 pt white or red wine, ½ pt fish fumet (see p. 23).

Season the salmon with salt and pepper. Smear the bottom of a pan generously with the butter, and cover with the carrot and onion and a bouquet garni. Cover the pan and braise it very slowly in a low oven for 15 minutes. Add the fish fumet (see p. 23), and wine so that there is enough liquid to half-cover the fish. Bring it to the boil and put it back in the oven. Cook for another 20 minutes, basting it frequently. Remove the salmon and serve either hot or cold with the cooking sauce.

Stuffed Salmon Cutlets

Stuff the salmon slices with a forcemeat fish stuffing, made with a mixture as in quenelles of pike (see p. 101). Then poach them and serve with a sauce nantua or mornay (see p. 171).

These can be made with small quantities of cooked salmon and can be served as an hors d'oeuvres or a main dish. Whether real scallop shells or the fire-proof kind are used, the method is the same.

Coquilles with Salmon

½ lb. flaked salmon with all bones and skin removed, ½ pt sauce, shrimps (optional garnish).

Cover the bottom of the shells with a tablespoon of the sauce and put the flaked salmon on top of that, cover with more of the sauce. Put the shells on a tin in a hot oven and brown quickly. Any of the sauces made with a béchamel base, such as mornay, are suitable. A few shrimps, or small pieces of shell fish, may be put on top of the salmon before pouring the sauce on top.

Other garnishes for coquilles, added before browning, are duxelles (see p. 86), with breadcrumbs and melted butter. Serve with chopped parsley and quartered lemons. These can also be eaten cold. Instead of sauce at the bottom, place some shredded lettuce or seasoned mixed vegetables like cooked, chopped carrots and peas, or French beans. Put the flaked salmon on top and cover with mayonnaise (see p. 171) or sauce verte (see p. 173).

In deference to its supposed Indian origin under the Raj, I include the curry powder, but I never use it myself.

Kedgeree of Salmon

1 lb. salmon poached, court bouillon or salted water, ½ lb. rice, 2

oz. butter, 1 tsp. curry powder (optional), 4 hard-boiled eggs, ½ pt sauce – white wine or cream sauce (see pp. 174, 168), 1 tbs. finely chopped parsley.

Cook the rice and flake the salmon, removing any bones and the skin. Warm the salmon gently in the butter with the curry powder, if liked. Chop up the hard-boiled eggs, but leave two of the yolks aside. Mix the rice, fish and hard-boiled egg together and season with the salt and pepper. Fold in the white wine or cream sauce. Chop the remaining 2 egg yolks very finely. Serve the kedgeree sprinkled with the egg yolks and the parsley. Equally good hot or cold. A tablespoon of very finely chopped mixed tarragon and chives can be added to the parsley.

Salmon Mousse

1 lb. salmon, 1 tsp. salt, large pinch of pepper, 4 egg whites, two of them whipped, juice of 1 lemon, 1 glass brandy, ¾ pt double cream, 1 oz. butter.

Pound raw or poached, diced salmon and season with salt and pepper; add only 2 whites of eggs. (This part of the cooking can be done in a blender as follows: put the diced salmon with the whites of egg and juice of lemon, a small glass of brandy, pepper and salt and blend until the mixture is very smooth.) Put the mixture on ice for 1 hour. Whisk the whipped cream into the fish mixture and then the 2 remaining stiffly beaten egg whites. Butter a soufflé dish and fill it with the mixture. Poach it in a bain-marie (pan of boiling water) then bake in a low oven (no. 3) for ¾–1 hour. Leave it to stand for 5–7 minutes before turning it out on to a heated serving dish. Serve with a green salad and cucumber.

Salmon Trout

Paler in colour, smaller but equally delicious, the salmon trout is in season from March to August. It can be cooked like river trout or like salmon, depending on its size.

Baked Salmon Trout

1 large or 2 small salmon trout weighing 2–2½ lb., salt, pepper, 8 oz. butter, cooking foil.

Season and spread the trout with softened butter. Butter the pieces of foil very generously and wrap each fish in a separate piece of foil. Leave enough to fold, so that all the juices are kept enclosed. Lay the fish on a rack in a baking tin and cook them in a medium oven (no. 4) for 25 minutes, depending on their size, up to about 35 minutes. Serve with the butter it was cooked in and quarters of lemon. New potatoes, young peas or salad go well with this dish. Salmon steaks or larger cuts may also be cooked in this way.

Try this first on salmon trout, as the result is more impressive if the fish is whole.

Salmon Trout in Aspic

1 poached salmon trout between 2–3 lb., ½ pt aspic jelly (see p. 165).

GARNISH

12 peeled prawns, 12 slices cucumber, lemon peel twists, truffles etc.

Poach the salmon trout (see p. 106). Allow the fish to drain and get cool. Remove the skin and put the salmon trout in the refrigerator. If the aspic jelly is prepared in advance, reheat it and then let it get cool again before spooning it over the salmon. While the jelly is cooling, decorate the fish with either prawns, sliced cucumber, truffles or any other garnish you like. Coat the garnish with the jelly. When the remainder of the aspic jelly is set hard, dice it with a sharp knife dipped in cold water. Surround the salmon trout with the aspic diced. When the glaze on the fish has set, it can be served, with either boiled or steamed potatoes or potato salad, and with mayonnaise.

Miscellaneous Fish Stews

Fish Stew with Red Wine

Allow 8 oz. fish for each person but the variety should include some trout, eel, perch and whatever else is available.

2 lb. mixed fish cut into chunks, 1 glass brandy, 2 chopped white part of leeks, 2 large onions chopped, 4 potatoes diced, 3 sticks coarsely chopped celery, bouquet garni, 4 crushed garlic cloves, 2 glasses burgundy, pepper, salt, 8–12 rounds toasted French bread rubbed with garlic, 1 oz. butter (optional).

Scale, clean, trim the fish and cut off their heads; cut them into chunks of equal size. Put all the pieces into an earthenware dish and sprinkle on a glass of brandy (not necessarily good quality), and allow to marinate for 2 hours. Sauté the vegetables in the butter, add 2 glasses burgundy, 4 crushed garlic cloves, salt and pepper. Simmer with the lid on for 30 minutes on top of the stove. Sieve this mixture and put the fish in it and cook with the lid on for 15–20 minutes, on a moderate heat. Rub the toasted bread with garlic, cut in 1-inch slices (assuming that this is French bread) and lay them at the bottom of a shallow dish or tureen. Put the fish on the toast and pour the sauce over it. If by any chance the sauce is too thin, thicken with a knob of beurre manié (see p. 22). A little butter added to the sauce will improve it too.

This is something that should be cooked, ideally, almost as soon as the fish are caught, and will appeal to those who like bouilla-baisse, and bourride and Mediterranean cooking.

Fish Stew (2)

2 lb. mixed fish in chunks, 2 large onions finely chopped, 4 crushed cloves garlic, bouquet garni, salt, pepper, 4 oz. butter, 1 glass brandy, 2 glasses red wine, ¼ lb. diced streaky bacon, 12 button onions, 4 oz. mushrooms, flour.

Prepare the fish as in the previous recipe for fish stew above. Put the butter into a flame-proof dish and add the onion, garlic, bouquet garni and fish. Season with salt and pepper. Heat the mixture until the fish pieces just stiffen, then flambé them with the brandy, add the wine, which should just cover the fish. Boil for 20 minutes. While the fish is cooking, fry the bacon and gently sauté the onions and mushrooms. Remove the pieces of fish and put them in the pan with the onions and mushrooms. Reduce the liquid from the fish cooking by half, and strain it into the second pan with the fish and bacon etc. Thicken it with a lump of beurre manié. Serve with croûtons fried in butter.

Flemish Fish Stew

Three or four varieties of fish, e.g. small carp, eel, perch, pike, are needed.

2 lb. mixed fish, salt, pepper, 4 parsley sprigs, 4 sticks celery.

Put the fish into a casserole with the seasoning and a bouquet of parsley and the celery. Cover with water, cook on a brisk fire for 20 minutes. Just before serving, add a tablespoon of dried bread crumbs or coarse matzo meal (see p. 91) to thicken the sauce.

Fur

Four-footed Game

Hare

It has never ceased to amaze me that hare ranks so low on the culinary scale in England. Presumably once an animal is classified as vermin it becomes damned for ever in English eyes. Luckily the hares don't seem to have been shamed out of existence and the French and Germans have benefited by large exports to them of our unwanted hares. Maybe the taste for them will come back slowly now that we have taken to drinking wine in increasing quantities and do not regard it as sinful to use in cooking. Perhaps economic circumstances will force the British to look favourably once more on that most versatile and delicious animal.

In the USA the hare is equally ubiquitous, but is usually called a Jack or Snowshoe Rabbit and, like its opposite number in Britain, is not confined to seasonal shooting. America, with its numerous minority groups, is fortunate in having such varied gastronomic traditions to call on. Central Europeans and Germans, in particular, have evolved some delicious recipes for hare, some of which I have included; my favourite among them is Hare with Walnuts.

Hares in England are in season from early August to the end of February, but as a rule they are at their best from October onwards. The brown or English hare is usually larger and more succulent than the blue Scottish specimen of the same age. Most obvious signs of youth or age are the hare's size and the yellowness of teeth. A young hare should have small white teeth, smooth coat, and claws well hidden by fur; it will probably weigh between six and seven pounds. But a fully grown hare over a year old will have yellowing teeth, slightly wavy fur, sometimes with greying in it, and large claws. Its weight can be as much as eleven or twelve pounds. If the hare looks as if it has been blasted by shot – reject it.

When dressed, hares lose about forty per cent of their weight. A leveret (young hare) of about four pounds dressed weight will feed four to six people well; a large hare is an excellent excuse for a dinner party of eight to ten people. Mature male hares are better marinated but the doe may well be tender – at least, up to about a year old – and can be prepared like a leveret. The latter will remain succulent if larded or wrapped in salt pork fat (barded) before cooking.

Although a raw hare cut up always looks an enormous quantity, it does shrink a good deal, especially with slow cooking.

Jugged hare or civet recipes often include the blood, so unless you are going to skin it and dress the hare yourself, ask the butcher to reserve it for you. Some shops sell joints of hare, so that you can buy only as much as you need. But if you are buying the entire hare, tell the butcher how you want it cut up if at all. Depending on the weather, a hare should be hung from seven to ten days. If the weather is cold and the hare is nice and fat, ten days is not too long, but in warm or damp weather, seven days is enough. Hang it head downwards with a bowl underneath to catch the blood. Good game dealers have a small bowl attached to the head for this, which gives the hare a strangely belligerent look. Hares are not paunched before they are hung.

An old hare will benefit from a couple of days marinating so that it should be skinned two days before you want to cook it. Some of the blood will have dripped out while it is hanging, but quite a lot more will still be inside the hare, so be prepared for a fairly bloody operation (see p. 116).

In general, young hare does not need marinating and can be roasted if it is lubricated with enough fat. But a little marinating in a small glass of brandy, even for young hare, can give a delicious flavour to the roast.

Hares over a year old not only need marinating for tenderizing but will absorb the flavours from the marinade. Better to roast only the *saddle* or *râble* (back legs plus saddle) of a mature hare, and casserole the other bits. I am against serving the head in roast hare as it is uncannily like having a death's head at the table. So if you intend to stuff the hare remove the head, and leave a good long flap of flesh to turn down for trussing. After you've stuffed it, as the individual recipes indicate, sew it up sufficiently to stop the filling oozing out.

Average times for roasting young hare vary from 18–20 minutes per pound in a hot oven, 20–22 minutes on the spit; for slow cooking, between 1½ and 2 hours.

As for the older hare, a good general rule to follow is that the older the hare the stronger the marinade and the longer the immersion. Barding, or larding, and long, slow cooking are the most likely methods to produce delicious results. Marinades need not always be the same; they can be varied by changing the herbs, spices, aromatics, in fact, almost all the ingredients. However, some sort of acid liquid is almost essential, whether it is wine, vinegar, lemon or cider – olive oil is often used and certainly helps to lubricate the flesh.

Preparation of Hare and Rabbit

Allow as much space as you can if you are doing the skinning and dressing yourself, and put down lots of old newspaper. A good, very sharp little knife for the incisions and a large knife or poultry shears for the jointing, if it is wanted, are necessary. You will also need a large, flat surface or a chopping board to rest the hare on.

Skinning

Cut off the four feet at the first joint, and make a light incision in the skin of one of the back legs. Pull the skin gently away from the flesh towards the head. Do the same with the other leg, and the same starting at the forelegs. At some point you will have to cut the hare up the middle to eviscerate it. Most of the blood will have collected in the chest cavity above the diaphragm, so be careful to collect this for appropriate recipes. (A teaspoon of vinegar will stop it coagulating.) When eviscerating hare, take the greatest care not to break the gall bladder. Keep the liver and kidneys aside. Now it is possible to separate the skin from the rather thin flesh from the belly of the hare. Continue the skinning until you get it right over the head. Obviously this will take a little time to start with, but will become easier as you get more confident. If you want to keep the head on for roasting a whole hare, there is no reason not to, but it is really worth more for stock-making. Wipe off the moisture from the outside and inside once you have removed all the blood. Personally, I prefer to rinse the hare quickly in cold water and dry it with a kitchen paper or cloth. The next thing is to remove the bluish membrane, especially from the saddle and back legs. The thin flesh from the belly is also better kept for stock but if you propose stuffing and roasting the hare, keep the skin round the belly intact but remove the outer membrane.

Trussing

To bring the back and forelegs close to the body and towards each other, cut the sinews at the joints. Use a trussing needle or fine skewers and secure with string.

Jointing

Cut off the legs either with poultry shears or sharp knife, cut the saddle into two or three pieces, by placing the knife on the backbone and giving it a smart tap with a hammer or other heavy weight. Cut off the ribs and head, which can be used for stock.

Rabbits are usually sold paunched (drawn), but if it has to be drawn, do it the same way as described for hare.

Recipe

A good basic marinade is as follows :

Red Wine Marinade

2 glasses red wine, 4 tbs. olive oil, 1 sliced onion, 1 clove garlic, 6 juniper berries, ¼ tsp. thyme or marjoram, 4 crushed peppercorns, 1 tsp. salt.

Instead of wine, cider or wine vinegar may be substituted, or lemon juice (as in Sicilian Hare).

For a young hare, a marinade of three tablespoons of brandy and three of olive oil, and various herbs and spices, is very good.

A simple roasting method when a hare is young and plump.

Roast Saddle of Hare

A saddle of hare weighing about 2 lb., 2 oz. butter, 8 strips pork fat, 2 glasses red wine, salt, pepper. (If the saddle is not large enough, the back legs can be left on.)

Remove the membrane from the hare and lard it with the pork strips evenly spaced, and sprinkle with freshly-ground pepper. Melt the butter and brush the hare with some of it, before roasting it in a moderately hot oven (no. 5-6) for about 45 minutes. (Allow another 10 minutes for spit roasting at the same temperature.) Baste the hare frequently during cooking with the remains of the melted butter and one glass of wine. When it is ready, put the carved hare in a serving dish at the bottom of the oven, turned down to no. 2. Pour off the fat from the pan and add the other glass of wine, mixing the cooking juices and wine evenly on a brisk fire while it reduces a little. Season with salt and more pepper if necessary, and serve this sauce separately. If the saddle has been adequately basted during cooking, the meat should be succulent but not bloody. Cranberry or red-currant preserve and baked jacket potatoes go well with this dish.

This method can be used when a hare is past its first youth.

Roast Saddle of Hare with Cream

1 saddle of hare, 2 oz. butter, 2 tbs. cognac, ¼ pt cream.

MARINADE

2 glasses red wine, 2 cloves garlic, bouquet garni, salt, pepper, 1 tsp. oregano.

Marinate the saddle in the red wine, garlic, bouquet garni, oregano, salt, and pepper for 4 hours. Drain and dry it before cooking. Pour the melted butter on to the saddle and cook for 15 minutes in a hot oven (no. 8). Warm the strained marinade, reduce the oven heat to no. 6 and baste the hare often. Cook for another 25 minutes. Flame the hare with cognac, carve into fillets, and keep warm on a serving dish. Pour the pan juices into a saucepan, heat, and add the cream. Cook quickly until it all thickens. Pour the sauce over the hare and serve with rice or noodles.

Stuffed Roast Hare

A young hare, 4 thin slices salt pork fat, 2 oz. butter.

STUFFING

4 oz. breadcrumbs, 2 finely chopped shallots, 2 oz. butter, hare liver, 1 tsp. oregano and thyme mixed together, 1 egg, salt and pepper.

Mince or pound the hare's liver with the shallots. Mix these with the other ingredients and bind with the egg. Stuff the hare and sew it up. Tie the slices of fat on and roast for about 1 hour in oven (no. 5). Baste frequently during cooking with butter and melted fat.

An alternative stuffing can be made with 4 oz. of very tender, minced rump steak, instead of the hare's liver. Onions can be used instead of shallots, if necessary. Garnish with watercress and horse-radish sauce, beetroot, or red-currant jelly. Serve with roast potatoes and a green salad.

Saddle of Hare with Mustard

Saddle and back legs of a young hare, 3 thin slices pork fat, ½ wine glass olive oil, 2 tbs. flour, 1 tbs. French mustard, 1 tbs. tomato purée, ½ wine glass cream.

MARINADE

3 glasses white wine, 1 glass wine vinegar, 2 sliced carrots, 3 small onions sliced, bouquet garni, 4 crushed peppercorns.

Remove the membrane from the hare and joint it. Marinate for 4 hours. Drain and dry the hare, tie on the fat securely and sprinkle on the flour. Brown the hare slowly in the olive oil in a heavy casserole, strain half the marinade on to it as well as the tomato purée. Simmer for 1 hour with the lid on. Add more of the marinade if the sauce evaporates too much during cooking. When the meat is tender, keep it hot on a serving dish. Mix the mustard with the cream and add it to the sauce. Pour over the hare and serve.

Casserole of Hare with Chestnuts

1 6-lb. hare, cut into serving pieces, 4 oz. diced streaky bacon, 12 button onions, 1 tbs. flour, salt and pepper, ½ bottle red wine, bouquet garni, 1 clove garlic, ½ lb. chestnuts, 1 pt stock (optional).

MARINADE

2 tbs. olive oil, 1 small glass brandy or armagnac, 2 large onions sliced.

Marinate the hare for at least 4 hours, turning the pieces fre-quently. While the hare is marinating, cook the skinned chestnuts in stock or salted water and brown the bacon lightly in the butter with the small onions in a large shallow pan. When the bacon is beginning to brown, add the drained pieces of hare and brown them lightly on all sides. Sprinkle on the flour and cook for another 5 minutes. Add the bouquet and a clove of garlic, and the red wine, which should cover all the pieces of hare. Cook with the lid on the pan in a slow oven for 3 hours. Put in the chestnuts, cook for another 10 minutes, remove bouquet and serve. Red cabbage is a good accompaniment.

Saddle of Hare with Chestnuts

1 saddle young hare, 2 mild bacon rashers, 3 oz. butter, 1 glass white wine, ¼ pt cream, 4 oz. chestnut purée, pepper and salt.

Smear the saddle thickly with the butter, wrap the bacon round it and sprinkle with pepper before covering in foil. Roast in a rather hot oven (no. 6–7) for about 45 minutes. When it is cooked keep hot on a serving dish. Pour off the excess fat from the roasting pan and add the white wine. Mix the cream and chestnut purée and add it to the sauce. Heat this together in the roasting pan on top of the stove.

Slice the saddle and pour the sauce over it. Serve with plain, green salad.

Hare in Walnut Sauce

1 hare, 3 oz. butter, 2 tbs. olive oil, small glass brandy, 1 pt meat stock, 1 oz. flour, large pinch cinnamon, bay leaf, salt and pepper, 6 slices bread, 12 walnuts, parsley.

MARINADE

3 sticks celery, 1 lemon, ½ cup vinegar, ½ cup water, marjoram.

Marinate the pieces of hare for 1 or 2 days in water, with vinegar, chopped celery, ½ the lemon cut up and the marjoram. Before cooking, dry the hare. Brown it lightly in the heated butter and olive oil, pour in the brandy and the juice of the remaining ½ lemon, and simmer the mixture for 15 minutes. Next add the heated stock, cinnamon, salt, pepper, and bay leaf. Cover tightly and cook for at least 2 hours very gently. Meanwhile, pound the walnuts and add them, together with the flour to the sauce 10 minutes before serving. Continue cooking until the sauce thickens. Fry the bread in the remaining butter and serve the hare on them. Garnish with crisp, fresh parsley. Serve with green salad of endive or lettuce.

Silesian Hare

1–2 saddles of hare, 8 slices mild bacon or salt pork, 3 dessertspoons olive oil, 3 sliced onions, 1 sliced carrot, 1 stick celery chopped, 1 white of leek, 5 juniper berries, 1½–2 pts meat stock, cornflour, ½ cup sour cream, juice of 1 lemon, 1 glass white wine, pepper, salt.

Tie salt pork securely round saddles and brown in olive oil in a heavy casserole. Add the vegetables and seasoning. Cook with the lid on in a medium oven for ½–¾ hour, preferably until the meat is still just pink. Remove the hare, and keep it warm in the oven. Cook the juices for about 5 minutes, add stock and simmer for 20 minutes. Strain and thicken with cornflour, stir in the cream and bring to the boil. Add the lemon juice and white wine. Divide the hare into serving portions with the bacon or salt pork. Pour some of the sauce over the hare on the dish, and serve the remainder separately. Boiled potatoes or noodles go well with this dish.

Hare Casserole with Caraway

1 hare cut up into twice the number of pieces usual when jointing it, 2 bay leaves, ½ tsp. caraway seeds, 2 sliced onions, 1 sliced carrot, 2 sliced sticks celery, 6 juniper berries, salt, pepper, 2 oz. beef dripping, 12 button onions, chopped cloves garlic, 1 tbs. flour, 1 glass red wine.

Simmer the pieces of hare in a saucepan in enough boiling water to cover them, with the vegetables, bay leaves, ½ teaspoon caraway seeds, juniper berries, salt and pepper. Two hours should be long enough for the meat to be tender and come away easily from the bones. When the hare is nearly cooked, start frying the button onions and the garlic in the dripping. When the meat is cool, strip it off the bones, sprinkle with flour and add it to the onions in the pan. When the meat and onions are brown, add a glass of red wine and stir this about with the hare and onions. When the sauce has thickened, the hare is ready to serve. If the wine is not sufficient to make the sauce, add a little of the stock. Red cabbage makes an excellent accompaniment to this dish.

Stewed Hare with Sultanas and Almonds

1 small hare, ¼ lb. diced bacon, 1 tbs. olive oil, 1½ oz. butter, salt and pepper.

MARINADE

2 glasses red wine, 1 oz. sultanas, ½ lemon-peel chopped, 1 oz. blanched almonds finely chopped, ½ tsp. ground nutmeg, 2 cloves, 1 apple cut into small pieces.

Marinate the jointed hare for 6–8 hours. Dry the hare, sprinkle with flour and brown in the mixture of oil and butter, with the bacon. Add all the marinade, salt and pepper. Cover the casserole tightly and simmer very slowly for 3 hours. Add a little more wine or water if the sauce gets too thick. Serve with rice, polenta (see p. 163) or buckwheat (see p. 160).

A simple dish of hare for eating on winter evenings when its voluptuous flavours will remind you of Mediterranean islands. The garlic's pungent flavour disappears in the slow cooking.

Sicilian Hare

1 4-lb. hare, 1 large sliced onion, ½ pt olive oil, 16 cloves garlic, 8 crushed juniper berries, 1 large glass red wine, 1 glass chicken or meat stock.

MARINADE

Juice of 6–8 lemons depending on size, 1 tbs. olive oil, oregano, salt and pepper.

Marinate the pieces of hare in an earthenware dish with the lemon juice, a tablespoon of olive oil, a teaspoon of oregano, salt and pepper, for at least 12 hours. Drain and dry the hare; pour the oil into a heavy saucepan and when it is bubbling hot add the sliced onion and brown lightly. Then brown the hare on both sides; add all the garlic cloves, a good sprinkling of oregano and the juniper berries, the stock and the wine. Cover tightly and simmer for about 3 hours. Serve with mashed potatoes, croûtons (see p. 17).

Hare with Sweet Pepper and Olives

1 hare, 8 strips pork fat, 1 tbs. olive oil, 1 oz. butter, 3 red or green sweet peppers, 6 tomatoes cut into large pieces, 16 green or black olives.

MARINADE

1 glass each of white wine and white wine vinegar, juice of 1 orange, ½ tsp. dried marjoram or tbs. fresh, 1 large sliced onion, 2 cloves garlic.

Lard the pieces of hare with the strips of fat and marinate in the mixture of wine vinegar, herbs and flavourings. Brown the hare in the mixture of oil and butter and then add the entire marinade. Cook slowly in a tightly covered casserole for an hour. Add the pimentos and ½ hour later, the tomatoes and cook for an additional 30 minutes. If the gravy is too thin, remove the hare and keep warm in the oven. Reduce the gravy to the consistency of a thinnish purée. Add the olives shortly before serving.

Hare with Celery

1 saddle of hare, 2 tbs. olive oil, 3 tbs. very rich stock, 1 tbs. red-currant jelly, ½ tsp. mustard, 6 slices white bread.

MARINADE

1 glass each white wine and white wine vinegar, 2 sliced carrots, 1 large onion sliced, 2 cloves garlic, bouquet garni, 4 crushed pepper-corns, salt.

Marinate the saddle of hare for about 48 hours. Turn it often so that all parts are equally soaked. Before cooking, dry the saddle. Heat the oil until it just begins to smoke in a sauté pan and brown the hare in it briefly for about 15 minutes leaving the flesh inside undercooked. Remove it from the fat but keep it hot. Reduce the strained marinade by about half, add the stock, a tablespoon of red-currant jelly and a little mustard, and cook for 3–4 minutes. Slice the saddle and place the slices in a fire-proof dish. Strain the sauce over the hare and cook the fillets for about 5 minutes, so that they are just cooked through. If necessary, thicken the sauce with a knob of beurre manié (see p. 22). Decorate the dish with croûtons. Serve with a celery purée (see p. 161).

Hare with Prunes

1 hare jointed (the blood, optional), 2 oz. butter, 2 tbs. gin, 1 tbs. flour, 4 glasses white wine or cider, 1 cup stock, 1 cupful prunes, 6 juniper berries, bay leaf, ½ tsp. marjoram.

MARINADE

1 glass red wine, 2 tbs. olive oil, 1 clove garlic, 6 crushed juniper berries, salt, pepper.

Marinate the hare pieces for 12 hours; soak the prunes. Drain and dry the pieces of hare and brown them in the butter in a heavy pan. Flame the hare with gin and sprinkle on the flour. Add the white wine or cider and stock and let this cook gently for 45 minutes with the lid on. Add the prunes and the strained marinade and cook for another 25 minutes or until the meat is tender. Just before serving, mix the blood of the hare with a little of the sauce. Pour back in the pan and heat for another 5 minutes. Serve on a purée of potato, or chestnut or parsnip.

A dish which is improved by adding the hare's blood.

Jugged Hare

1 small hare cut into serving pieces, 16 button onions, 6 oz. mild streaky bacon, 2 oz. butter, 1 tbs. olive oil, 1 oz. flour, ½ pt red burgundy, 2 tbs. tomato purée, 4 oz. mushrooms, bouquet garni, hare's blood.

To prevent the blood of the hare coagulating, add 1 tablespoon vinegar to it. Peel the onions, dice the bacon, and sauté them gently in the butter in a heavy, metal casserole. When they are lightly browned, take them out and keep aside. Brown the pieces of hare all over in the same fat and then sprinkle the flour on. Add the bouquet, wine, and, if necessary, water, so that all the hare is covered. Add the tomato purée and season. Simmer gently in the covered casserole for 1½–2 hours – the hare should be tender by this time. Remove the pieces to a fire-proof serving dish and keep warm with a lid on. Add to the sauce in which the hare was cooked, the onions, mushrooms and bacon, and simmer gently for another 10–15 minutes, so that the vegetables are cooked. Remove 3 tbs. of the sauce from the casserole and add it drop by drop to the blood; when it is all mixed together, pour it back into the casserole and cook gently to avoid curdling for another 10 minutes until the entire sauce thickens. With this rather rich sauce only a very bland vegetable or rice should be served.

Casserole of Hare

1 young hare cut into serving pieces, ¼ lb. slice of mild streaky bacon or salt pork, 12 button onions, 12 pitted black olives.

MARINADE

½ bottle vin rosé, salt, 4 crushed peppercorns, 4 crushed juniper berries, 1 bouquet with marjoram added, 1 large sliced onion, 3 crushed garlic cloves.

Marinate the hare in an earthenware dish overnight. Drain the pieces of hare. Dice the pieces of bacon or pork and let them melt gently with the button onions which should brown very slightly. Take the bacon and onions out of the pan and keep aside. Brown the hare pieces in the bacon fat. Meanwhile, warm the marinade and add all of it to the casserole, cover closely and simmer for 1 hour. Remove all the solid ingredients from the original marinade with a perforated ladle and put in the little onions, bacon and black olives. Serve with a sprinkle of chopped parsley. Use bread or potato purée to absorb the sauce.

A legendary recipe from France.

Civet de Lièvre de Diane de Châteaumorand

A hare, 1 onion, 1 oz. pork fat diced, 2 oz. butter, 1 oz. flour, ½ cup meat stock, ½ glass red wine, salt and pepper, blood and liver of hare.

MARINADE

1 small glass wine vinegar, ½ wine glass olive oil, 3 sprigs thyme, 1 sliced onion.

Marinate the hare pieces in the wine vinegar, olive oil, thyme and 1 sliced onion for 12 hours at least. Turn the hare periodically so that all the pieces are thoroughly permeated by the marinade. Chop the remaining onion and the pork fat and put into a heavy pan. Add the strained and dried hare and sauté the pieces on a low heat in the butter, with the lid on for 20 minutes. Dust with the flour and continue cooking slowly for another 20 minutes. Turn it about frequently. Now add the stock, red wine and seasoning before simmering for another 40 minutes. While the hare is cooking, pound the liver with the strained marinade and the blood of the hare to a paste. When the hare is cooked, put it on a serving dish and keep warm. Five minutes before serving bring the cooking liquid to the boil and add the paste of liver, more seasoning if necessary, and a teaspoon of vinegar. Finally, pour in a teaspoon of olive oil and mix well. Serve with boiled potatoes or croûtons, or just crisp French bread.

The saucisson d'Arles, which is highly seasoned, gives a delicious flavour to the fillet.

Hare à L'Arlésienne

Saddle and back legs of hare, 6 slices of Arles sausage, 4 tbs. olive oil, 1 glass of wine, 2 tbs. tomato purée, 1 clove garlic, 1 tsp. freshly chopped thyme, 6 slices white bread, 2 oz. butter, 1 tbs. chopped parsley, salt, pepper.

Cut from the saddle and back legs as many thickish slices as you can – there should be at least 8. Then cut each sausage slice into 4. Make a cut in each hare fillet into which you firmly press the piece of sausage. Sauté the fillets for about 25 minutes in the oil, making sure they are cooked, but do not let them get dry. When they are almost cooked, add the warmed wine, the tomato purée, the thyme and the garlic. Cover the pan and simmer for another 10 minutes. Meanwhile, fry the bread in butter. Serve the hare fillets covered with the sauce on the croûtons. Add salt and pepper if necessary, but the sausage should give adequate flavouring. Sprinkle with the parsley. If you cannot get the saucisson d'Arles, bacon will do but the result will not be quite as good. You will need more seasoning of salt and pepper.

Hare Pie

1 small hare, 1 sliced carrot, 2 onions sliced, bay leaf, salt and pepper, 2 glasses port, 1 lb. puff pastry.

Have the hare cut into small pieces, not the usual joints. Put the pieces in a heavy stewpan with the onions, carrots, bay leaf and seasoning. Cook gently for about 3 hours. Put the pieces of hare into a pie dish. Reduce the cooking liquid so that it almost covers the hare, add 2 glasses of port and correct the seasoning. Cover with puff pastry and bake about ½ hour in a hot oven.

Made with the remains of a large hare when only the saddle has been cooked.

Terrine of Cooked Hare

Pieces of hare, ½ bottle red burgundy, 2 onions, 3 cloves garlic, 1 bay leaf, 1 tbs. oregano or marjoram, ½ lb. unsmoked streaky bacon diced.
1 tbs. marjoram, 1 crushed clove garlic, pepper, salt, nutmeg, 6–8 rashers very mild streaky bacon.

1ST STAGE (for making a terrine or pâté)

Put the hare into a casserole with red wine, sliced onions, 3 garlic cloves, bay leaf, and oregano and diced bacon. Cover and cook for ¾–1 hour in a medium oven. When the hare is tender strain off the liquid and keep it aside. As soon as the meat is cool, take it off the bones and mince it with the bacon.

2ND STAGE

Add the second lot of herbs and garlic, freshly milled pepper and salt, if necessary. On the bottom of a 2-pint terrine, put a layer of the bacon rashers then a thick layer of the hare and finish with bacon rashers at the top. Pour on the original cooking liquid reduced so that the hare mixture is moist. Put a layer of foil or greaseproof paper over the terrine, stand it in a pan of water (bain-marie) and cook in a cool oven (no. 2) for 2 hours. The terrine should be cooked when the fat on top looks quite clear.

Allow the terrine to cool with a slight weight on it. It will improve the flavour if it is kept in a refrigerator for 2 or 3 days. Before storing, cover the terrine with melted lard. Cover the cold terrine with foil when you keep it, as the smell will penetrate into all the other food in the refrigerator.

Terrine of Uncooked Hare

1 hare, 1 lb. salt pork fat in thick strips, 1 glass brandy, 1 lb. finely-minced pork, 8–10 mild bacon rashers, 4 crushed juniper berries, pepper, salt, 2 cloves garlic, 1 tsp. thyme, pinch of nutmeg, 1 glass of red wine, 2 or 3 bay leaves.

Remove as much meat from the saddle, back legs and forelegs as possible. Slice into strips and put these with the salt pork strips into a small dish and marinate them with the brandy for 4 hours. Mix the finely minced pork with the marinated hare and all the herbs and spices; line the terrine with the bacon rashers, and alternate layers of the hare and pork mixture and bacon, finishing with a layer of bacon on top covered with the bay leaves. Cover with foil, put on the lid and cook in a bain-marie (see p. 27), for 2½–3 hours, in a medium oven. The proportions of hare meat to pork should be approximately 2 to 1 – otherwise your terrine will be somewhat characterless. If the bacon rashers are too strong or salt, they will give the terrine an over-obtrusive flavour of bacon.

A slight variation in appearance and flavour can be obtained by alternating layers of marinated hare only with hare and pork mixture and layers of bacon.

Hare Pâté
Stage 1 as in Terrine of Cooked Hare (p. 127).

To make a pâté proper, which is just a terrine surrounded by a pastry, it is essential to have a hinged mould. For the terrine already described, line a mould with pastry about ½-inch thick. Fill it with a mixture of hare etc. and cover it with a pastry lid. Let it stand for an hour before cooking. Brush the pastry with a little yolk of egg to give it a glaze. Cook it in the oven no. 5 with a china pastry chimney to let the steam escape.

Hare Brawn

1 small hare, 1 lb. shoulder of gammon, 2 onions, salt, pepper, bouquet garni, 1 lb. chopped veal bones, 4 peppercorns, 1 tbs. capers.

Marinate the cut-up hare for 8–12 hours in the marinade on. p. 117. Soak the gammon for 2 hours to remove excess salt. Cook the hare, gammon and veal bones covered in water with the vegetables and bouquet for 2 hours very slowly. Remove all the meats and allow the stock to reduce by half. When the meats are cool, strip off all the meat from the hare and cut it and all the gammon into smallish pieces. Mix them in a dish with the meat broth and the capers. Place in a wetted mould or pudding basin and pour on the very reduced stock. Press down, cover with a plate and put a weight on it. Keep in the refrigerator, till set. Serve it with salads such as Russian, potato, green or mixed salad.

Rabbit

There are wild rabbits and domesticated rabbits, and though the farmed rabbit is more tender, it is less gamey in flavour. For culinary purposes the recipes can be used equally on both sorts, but the marinades and the strongly flavoured dishes are more rewarding when wild rabbits are used.

There is no close season for shooting rabbits as farmers detest them, but despite the efficiency of mechanical farming, which leaves little corn for the rabbits to get fat on, they seem to survive. Even the officially approved myxomatosis has failed to exterminate them, and now a new immunized breed is emerging. In Europe the rabbit is not sneered at as a dish (or fed to cats and dogs as is often the case in England). In the United States rabbit is called hare in certain parts, just as hare is called Jack rabbit.

The rabbit which has been living on a varied diet of young green shrubs and fattening corn will provide the best-flavoured flesh. Harvest time, whenever that is in the different countries, is the best time to eat them.

Young rabbits have smooth claws, soft thin ears which tear easily and small, white teeth. They are delicious roast, grilled or fried. Old rabbits should be given prolonged cooking or marinading or both. They should both, that is young and old alike, be fresh; one day's hanging in a cool, dry place will be enough for a wild rabbit. Paunch (remove entrails and stomach) before hanging by the legs. If the liver is needed for the recipe and it looks a healthy colour, keep it; if not, throw it away. (For further information on the preparation of rabbit see pp. 116, 117.)

One young rabbit is barely enough for three people. Allow two for four people, and use any left-overs in pies or terrines. Allow forty-five minutes on average for roasting and 1½–2 hours for casseroles and slow methods of cooking.

Roast Rabbit

2 young rabbits, 1 cup made mustard, 1 lb. thin rashers streaky bacon, black pepper, 2 oz. butter.

Truss the rabbit covering it thickly with a coating of mustard and wrap it entirely in thin rashers of streaky bacon. Place on the rack in a roasting pan and cook in the oven on no. 4 for 1 hour, basting frequently with melted butter. Serve with the cooking juices poured over it. Baked or roast potatoes and salad go well with this dish.

For very young, tender rabbits only.

Grilled Rabbit

1 young rabbit, 2 pts salted water, 2 oz. butter, pepper, salt, 2 tbs. French mustard, 1 tbs. cream.

Cut the rabbit down the middle, trimming off the ribs, and make several cuts across the back so that it can lie flat. Let it soak in salted water for an hour with a weighted plate on it. Take it out, wipe it dry and cover it with melted butter on both sides. Season with pepper and salt. Cook under a moderately hot grill for 10 minutes either side, turning twice during cooking, and basting frequently with melted butter. Before serving, mix 2 teaspoons of French mustard with the cream and put it under the grill again for 5 minutes. Serve with sauté potatoes and green salad.

Roast Stuffed Rabbit

1 rabbit, 3 slices fat salt pork, 2 oz. butter, 1 glass white wine, flour, salt, pepper.

MARINADE

1 glass wine, red or white, 1 sliced carrot, onion, 1 clove garlic, 1 bouquet garni, ½ glass wine vinegar.

STUFFING

½ lb. finely minced pork, salt, pepper, ½ tsp. mixed basil and oregano.

Marinate the rabbit for 8 hours turning occasionally. Drain and dry the rabbit and tie on the slices of bacon. Stuff the rabbit with the forcemeat and sew it up. Truss it and spread with melted butter. Put on a roasting rack in a hot oven (no. 5) and cook for 1 hour, basting frequently with melted butter and the strained marinade. Thicken the pan juices with a dessertspoon of flour, add a glass of white wine and pepper and salt. Before serving, remove the bacon slices and pour the sauce over the rabbit. Baked potatoes and a green salad are good accompaniments. Apple sauce adds a fresh piquant touch.

Pot Roast Rabbit

See Pigeon (p. 60).

Rabbit à l'Espagnole

1 jointed rabbit, ¼ pt olive oil, 2 oz. pork fat or lard, 2 chopped cloves of garlic, 1 bay leaf, 1 tbs. parsley chopped, 1 clove, 1 glass white wine, 1 oz. cooking chocolate, 1 tumbler water, pepper, salt.

Take a heavy saucepan and brown the rabbit pieces in oil and lard; add the garlic, bay leaf, parsley, clove, white wine and chocolate. Stir the rabbit pieces around so that they are all equally covered with the mixture. Season with pepper and salt and add the water. Cover with the lid and simmer on top of the stove for 1¼ hours. Serve from the casserole with a purée of celery or turnip or with rice.

Fried Rabbit (1)

8 small fleshy pieces of rabbit, 2 eggs, pepper and salt, 2 cups very fine breadcrumbs, handful of parsley, 2 lemons.

Soak the rabbit in moderately salted water for 2–3 hours at least. Beat the egg, season with pepper and salt. Dry the rabbit pieces after its preliminary soaking, dip the pieces into the breadcrumbs, then into the egg, twice. Heat some corn or nut oil in a deep frying pan (or one that is especially kept for deep frying, with a wire basket). When the oil starts to smoke, drop the rabbit pieces in one by one. (If all the pieces are put in together it will lower the temperature of the oil, so that the egg and breadcrumbs will become a soggy mess.) Lower the heat and cook for 15–20 minutes. The fierce heat will ensure that the rabbit is cooked and the egg and breadcrumbs makes a crunchy protective coating. If you are doubtful about the rabbit pieces being thoroughly cooked by this method, fry the rabbit pieces first so that they are three-quarters cooked, then egg and breadcrumb them.

When the rabbit is well browned, remove it from the oil and put the pieces on some kitchen paper to absorb any fat surplus. Serve on a heated dish, garnish with sprigs of parsley and quartered lemons. A crisp salad is really all that is needed but this is a dish where chips or sauté potatoes do nothing to detract from it.

After coating the pieces of rabbit (or any game) preparatory to frying, let the pieces stand for 30 minutes, or thereabouts, to tighten up before frying. Some cooks prefer to flour the pieces of meat before dipping them into the beaten egg or milk and then roll them in the breadcrumbs. However, if the breadcrumbs are very fine, this should not be necessary.

A young rabbit is essential to this as it is a quickly cooked dish.

Fried Rabbit (2)

4 pieces of saddle of rabbit, 1 egg yolk, 1 cup breadcrumbs.

MARINADE

2 tbs. wine vinegar, 1 tbs. olive oil, one sliced onion, bay leaf, 2 sprigs parsley, 1 tsp. lemon juice.

Marinate the pieces of rabbit for 1 hour, then drain and dry them. Dip them twice in the seasoned egg and breadcrumbs and fry them for 20 minutes in butter on a moderate heat. Turn at least twice during cooking. Serve with a sauce tartare (see p. 173).

A slight variation is to season the fine breadcrumbs with finely chopped parsley, grated lemon rind, marjoram, thyme, salt and pepper.

Braised Rabbit

1 jointed rabbit, 3 chopped shallots, 3 sliced carrots, 1 small glass brandy or gin, 2 chopped garlic cloves, 4 crushed juniper berries, 6 coriander seeds, salt and pepper, 1 dessertspoon flour, 1 glass red wine.

Brown the vegetables very slowly in the mixed oil and butter; take them out of the pan while the rabbit is browning in the same fat. Put back the vegetables, lay the rabbit on top and flame it with a small glass of brandy or gin. Add the garlic, juniper berries and coriander. Cover with foil and the lid, and cook slowly on top of the stove for 1 hour. When the rabbit is tender, put the pieces on a serving dish. Stir in the flour to the juices in the pan, add a glass of red wine and salt and pepper if needed. Strain the sauce over the rabbit and sprinkle freshly chopped parsley or mint over it. Serve with spinach or peas.

Rabbit with Tomato

1 young rabbit, 2 tbs. flour, ½ pt meat or poultry stock, 2 oz. butter or 2 tbs. beef dripping, ½ pt tomato purée preferably fresh, ½ tsp. sugar, salt and pepper, 2 tsp. fresh basil chopped.

Joint a young rabbit, sprinkle on the flour and brown the pieces in butter or beef dripping in a sauteuse. Add ½ pt stock. Reduce the heat, cover the pan and simmer for 45 minutes. Add ½ pt tomato purée and cook for 15 minutes, while the tomato purée amalgamates with the sauce in the pan. If it is too thick add a little stock to thin it to the right consistency. Stir the sauce while bringing it to the boil and add a pinch of sugar, season with salt and pepper. Serve in the sauteuse, sprinkle with finely chopped fresh basil. Serve with mashed potatoes, noodles or rice.

Not to put too fine a point on this recipe, it can be either the basis for paella, or without the shell fish and chorizos, a delicately flavoured rabbit dish. You will need either a paella pan, deep sauteuse, or deep frying-pan.

Rabbit with Saffron

1 young rabbit, cut into small pieces, 3–6 shreds of saffron according to taste, salt, pepper, a little marjoram or basil, 2 cups rice, 2 oz. butter, 3 tbs. olive oil, 1 pimento cut into strips.

PAELLA

3 chorizos, 12 mussels, 12 french beans, 12 prawns.

Fry the small rabbit pieces in the oil and butter very gently for 20 minutes, turning often so that they become brown and tender. Take out the pieces and fry 2 cups of either Valencia or Italian rice in the fat so that it all glistens. Add 6 cups of boiling water and 3–6 shreds of saffron, salt, pepper and a little marjoram or basil. Allow the rice to absorb all the liquid while the rabbit continues to cook with it. After 25 minutes, the rice should be almost cooked. Now add the strips of pimento. Let them cook for 5 minutes and serve with finely chopped parsley and quartered lemons.

To make a paella, add some cut-up chorizos (Spanish smoked sausages), chopped green beans, cleaned mussels, prawns or whatever your favourite paella ingredients are.

On the plateau of the second highest mountain, L'Offra, in Majorca, is a hunting lodge. In the garden there are the sweetest pimentos, tomatoes and courgettes, and rabbits and herbs abound on the mountain-side. The sun-ripened vegetables and fresh herbs make this dish special.

Majorcan Rabbit

2 young rabbits, 4 tbs. olive oil, 4 pimentos, 2 courgettes, 4 tomatoes.

MARINADE

2 glasses white wine, 2 cloves garlic, 1 sliced onion, salt, pepper, 3 sprigs wild thyme or marjoram.

Marinate the cut-up rabbit for 4 hours. Drain and dry and brown in the olive oil. Add the marinade, cover the pot and simmer for 30 minutes. Add the pimentos and courgettes and cook for another 10 minutes then add the tomatoes. Simmer for a further 15 minutes. Remove the lid and allow the liquid to reduce until the sauce is almost like a purée. Add more salt and pepper if needed. Eat with fresh crusty country bread and plenty of wine. A handful of black or green olives can be added to the dish 5 minutes before serving.

Rabbits in Cider or White Wine

8 small pieces rabbit, 3 oz. butter or dripping, 4 oz. diced bacon, ½ pt cider or 2 glasses white wine, salt, pepper, ½ tbs. marjoram, rabbit liver, 1 clove garlic, 1 cup fine breadcrumbs, ½ cup chopped parsley.

Brown the rabbit pieces in the fat with the diced bacon. Meanwhile, heat the cider and pour it over the rabbit; see that the rabbit is just covered with the cider, add salt, pepper and the marjoram. Simmer slowly for 1½ hours with the lid on. While the rabbit simmers crush the rabbit's liver with the garlic, add a ½ cup of breadcrumbs and chopped parsley. Add this thickish paste to the sauce 5 minutes before serving. Serve with peas or mushrooms, and potatoes, boiled or sautéed.

If white wine is preferred, boil it and pour it flaming over the rabbit.

If you can call Irish stew, ragoût Irlandais, without feeling silly, this would be called Lapin Irlandais.

Rabbit Hot Pot

1 jointed rabbit, 2 oz. butter, 3 large potatoes cut into thick slices, 3 sliced carrots, 3 leeks, pepper, salt, 1 lb. peas shelled, broad beans.

In a deep heavy metal casserole, brown the pieces of rabbit in the butter. Add the vegetables except peas and beans, season with pepper and salt and just cover all with boiling water. Simmer fairly quickly for 1½ hours. When the rabbit is tender, take it out and put it on a serving dish to keep warm in the oven. Strain the vegetables and purée them, and add a knob of butter, salt and pepper if necessary. Cook the peas and beans in the stock. Surround the rabbit with the puréed vegetables and the peas and beans. Other vegetables may be substituted for those mentioned, particularly parsnips, turnip, celery and onion. As rabbits take so well to garlic-flavoured vinaigrette sauce, it can be served cold with the sauce and plenty of chopped parsley, and if you have them, other mild fresh herbs.

Rabbit with Prunes

2 saddles or 1 large rabbit, 4 oz. butter, 2 tbs. flour, ½ pt stock, salt, pepper, 1 lb. stoned prunes, 1 tbs. red-currant jelly.

MARINADE

2 glasses red wine, ½ glass vinegar, 6 juniper berries, 1 clove garlic.

Marinate the pieces of rabbit for 24 hours. Drain and dry the rabbit and brown it well in the butter in a casserole. Stir the flour into the butter, add the stock and the marinade liquid gradually. Season with salt and pepper, put in the prunes and simmer for 1½ hours with the lid on (1 hour for a very young rabbit). Place the rabbit on a fire-proof serving dish surrounded by the prunes. Add the red-currant jelly to the sauce, stir well, bring to the boil and pour over the rabbit.

Instead of dried prunes, use dried apricots, sultanas, or a mixture of these dried fruits.

Rabbit with Tarragon

1 rabbit, pepper, salt, 2 tbs. flour, 2 oz. butter, 1 dessertspoon olive oil, 1½ glasses white wine, 1 tbs. chopped fresh tarragon, 1 chopped clove garlic, 1 tbs. meat jelly or rich stock.

A heavy shallow pan which will be big enough to sauté all the pieces is necessary. Sprinkle the cut-up rabbit with flour, pepper and salt, and brown it quickly in the mixture of olive oil and butter. Add 1 glass of white wine and garlic, lower the heat, cover the pan and simmer for 40 minutes. While the rabbit is cooking, soak the tablespoon of chopped tarragon in the remaining ½ glass of white wine. When the rabbit is tender, pour the wine and chopped tarragon over the rabbit. Turn all the pieces of rabbit so that the tarragon and garlic is evenly spread over them. Cook briskly with the lid on for another 7 minutes. Remove the rabbit on to a heated serving dish. Dilute the pan juices with a tablespoon of meat jelly or rich stock and pour it over the rabbit. Serve with braised celery, turnip purée, or Jerusalem artichokes. If no fresh tarragon is available, ½ teaspoon of dried should be used, but the result will not be quite so good.

Stifado or Estouffade of Rabbit

1 large rabbit cut up, 2 oz. butter, 2 tbs. olive oil, 4 large sliced Spanish onions, 1 large tin of tomatoes, 2 tbs. fresh chopped parsley, salt, pepper.

MARINADE

1 glass white wine, 2 tbs. olive oil, bouquet garni, 4 crushed juniper berries, 2 cloves garlic, pepper and salt.

Marinate the jointed rabbit for 4 hours; turn it about occasionally. Drain and dry the rabbit and brown it in the oil and butter, then take it out and keep aside. Brown the onions and return the rabbit to the saucepan. Boil the marinade and all its ingredients and pour it over the rabbit. Simmer for two hours on top of the stove. Add the strained tomatoes and cook rather more quickly for 15 minutes, stirring the sauce so that the tomatoes and onions and all the marinade ingredients amalgamate. By the time the rabbit is cooked, the onions and tomatoes etc., should have formed a thick purée. Take out the rabbit pieces, put them on a heated serving dish, and keep warm. Sieve the sauce over the rabbit through a fairly coarse wire sieve and add more seasoning if necessary. Sprinkle liberally with chopped parsley.

Most tinned tomatoes come from Mediterranean countries and tend to be sweeter than the English variety which makes them better suited to this recipe.

Rabbit in Egg and Lemon Sauce

1 rabbit, 1 tbs. salt, 4 oz. salt pork, 12 button onions, ¼ lb. sliced mushrooms, ½ lemon, bouquet garni, 6 peppercorns, salt, 2 oz. butter, 1 tbs. flour, 2 egg yolks, 2 tbs. cream, 2 pts slightly salted water.

Dice the salt pork, peel the onions and slice the mushrooms while the rabbit soaks in the salted water for 2 hours. Beat the egg yolks and add them to the cream with 2 teaspoons of lemon juice so that this is ready for the sauce. Put the rabbit, pork, onions, bouquet and a very small piece of lemon rind into a heavy stewpan. Cover with fresh cold water and bring it gently to the boil. Keep it bubbling until all the scum has been taken off. Reduce the heat and simmer gently with the lid on for an hour. When the rabbit is tender, put it with the pork and the onions on a dish to keep warm. Reduce the rabbit broth to two cupfuls and strain it. Make a roux (see p. 24) with the butter and flour and add, first, the reduced broth and then the beaten egg yolks and cream. Season with more salt and pepper if necessary. Pour the sauce over the rabbit, add the sliced mushrooms and heat up again gently before serving, either with rice or fluffy mashed potatoes.

Rabbit Marengo

1 rabbit cut in small pieces, 4 tbs. olive oil, pepper, salt, 1 lb. sliced mushrooms, 2 sliced truffles (if available), 1 tbs. chopped parsley, 2 tbs. fresh tomato sauce.

Soak the rabbit pieces in cold, salted water for 2 hours. Dry the rabbit and add them to the smoking hot oil in a sauteuse. Season with salt and pepper and cook quite briskly for 30 minutes with the lid on. Pour the oil the rabbit was cooked in into a small saucepan. Heat it well and add the mushrooms, parsley, truffles, and tomato sauce. Serve with the sauce poured over the rabbit on rice or noodles.

Uncle Sam Rabbit

1 large rabbit jointed, salt, pepper, 3 oz. butter, 2 sliced onions, 2 sliced carrots, ½ pt stock, 1 glass cider, 1 large tin whole sweet corn drained, fresh parsley, ½ cup cream.

Marinate the rabbit in salted water for 3 hours. Drain and dry. Brown the seasoned pieces of rabbit in a heavy casserole in the butter together with the onions and carrots. Add the stock and the cider. Cover with lid and simmer on a low fire for 1¼ hours. Fifteen minutes before serving, add the sweet corn and cream and heat gently together with the rabbit for 10 minutes. Serve the rabbit surrounded by the sweet corn and sprinkled with chopped parsley.

Rabbit Fricassée

1 rabbit jointed, 1 diced carrot, onion, turnip, 6 sprigs parsley, salt, pepper, 2 oz. butter, 2 tbs. flour, ½ cup milk, 1 cup stock. (Marinate an elderly rabbit in salt water and lemon juice or vinegar for 4 hours.)

Put the rabbit in a pan with the diced vegetables, season and cover with cold water. Simmer on a low heat for 1½–2 hours. Remove the rabbit from the pan and take all the meat off the bones. Make a white roux (see p. 24) from the butter and flour and add a cup of the rabbit stock and half a cup of milk and make a creamy sauce. Put the rabbit back into the sauce and reheat gently. Serve with rice, potatoes, or noodles, sprinkled liberally with fresh chervil, basil or parsley.

Rabbit Pie

1 boiled rabbit or remains of, ½–1 lb. finely minced pork, 2–4 hard-boiled eggs, pepper, salt, ¼ tsp. fresh thyme or ¼ tsp. dried thyme,

1 tbs. chopped parsley, 1 cup rabbit broth, ½–¾ lb. pastry, salt, pepper.

Put all the above ingredients, except the pastry, into a pie dish with the stock. Cover with the pastry and bake in a medium-hot oven for 45 minutes. Eat hot or cold and serve with salad or green vegetables.

On the Quai Stalingrad in Toulon there are, or were, many restaurants, some bad, some good, but in one of them I ate a terrine of rabbit. It was on my first visit to the South of France without an adult. I think it must have been that terrine that started my conscious interest in cooking. I remarked to the waiter that the terrine was delicious. Before we left the restaurant, the chef who was also the owner gave me the recipe; I think it was mainly from curiosity on his part to see a young English girl who was impressed with his cooking.

Terrine of Rabbit (1)

1½ lb. rabbit, 1 lb. belly of salt pork, 4 streaky bacon rashers, 3 cloves garlic, zest of lemon, 4 juniper berries, 1 tsp. fresh thyme or ¼ tsp. dried thyme, ¼ tsp. ground mace, pepper, salt, 1 liqueur glass cognac or other brandy, 2 bay leaves, 2 tbs. pork fat.

Blanch the rabbit for 5 minutes in boiling, salted water; drain and simmer the rabbit pieces again in fresh water for 25 minutes. When cool enough to handle, take all the meat off the bones. The rabbit should be cut very finely into strips. Chop the uncooked belly of pork very finely or mince it coarsely. Chop the garlic and lemon zest and crush the juniper berries. Add these to the mixed meats and season with the black pepper, mace, thyme and salt. Stir in the cognac and make sure that all the ingredients are evenly mixed together. Cut the bacon rashers into 3 strips and line the bottom of a 2-pt terrine with them; cover with a layer of the meat mixture. Put a couple of bay leaves on that and finish off with more strips of bacon. Cover the terrine with a lid and cook in a bain-marie in oven (no. 3) for 1½ hours. When the cooking is finished, take off the lid and place some greaseproof paper over the terrine with a weight on it. Leave it to set overnight. Cover with melted pork fat. The terrine will keep for several days in a refrigerator. Freshly chopped parsley sprinkled on when serving adds (for me an authentic) aromatic flavour. If 3 cloves of garlic seems excessive, I can only say that that is how it was in Toulon.

Terrine of Rabbit (2)

See Terrine of Hare (p. 127) and Terrine of Rabbit (1).

To make a terrine with uncooked rabbit meat, soak the rabbit pieces in plenty of slightly salted water. Dry the pieces and with a very sharp knife remove all the flesh from the bones. Cut the rabbit in very fine strips and marinate in the brandy for four hours. The bones can be kept for making game stock. Then proceed in exactly the same way as for the terrine made with cooked rabbit.

For a change, the terrine can be made with ½ lb. liver pâté instead of minced pork; but you will need rather more rabbit for a 2-pint terrine.

A cross between a thick soup and a stew for cooler evenings – simplicity itself to prepare.

Rabbit Soup Créole

2 young rabbits, cut into small pieces, 1 sliced onion, salt, pepper, pinch of cayenne pepper, ½ cup rice, 2 tbs. sherry, 1 blade of mace.

Put the rabbit pieces into a heavy pan with 2 pints of cold water. Add the chopped onion, a bay leaf and a blade of mace. Bring to the boil and simmer very gently for 2 hours. Add salt, pepper and a pinch of cayenne pepper as well and half a cup of rice. Simmer for another 30 minutes. Add 2 tablespoons of sherry before serving.

Venison

Long before I ever thought about writing this book, I had often asked English people if they liked venison. To my astonishment at least fifty per cent did not even know what it was. Now the Scots were different – many had eaten it and liked it in varying degrees, and had even seen it on sale in shops in Scotland. A Scots friend of mine, whose father supplied a good deal of the game for the top shops and hotels in London before the First World War, remembers how the markets in Dundee sold the remains of their cheapest cuts at three pence a pound on a Saturday night to those who had already spent the best part of their meagre wages in pubs. It is doubtful that these impoverished Scots knew the etymological origins of the word, but whatever they are, *venison* now applies almost exclusively to the flesh of the deer.

In Great Britain these are the red deer, the roe and the fallow deer. Most of the venison from the red deer comes from Scotland, and a good many of the roe as well. The fallow deer is quite common in England but I have heard them scathingly referred to by the buyer of an internationally known store as 'park deer', whose flavour has little in common, and is also vastly inferior to what he called 'real' venison. The buck (male) of any deer is thought to be better flavoured than the doe (female) but I would say that depended a lot on its age. The optimum age for deer is between 18 months and 2 years old.

In America venison also includes the flesh of the elk, the moose and the Caribou reindeer, which are found in many of the different States, though the latter are largely confined to Alaska, which may well of course soon become quite thickly populated (by humans, I mean, not deer).

Like the laws that apply to all other game, these vary from State to State with regard to deer as well. Much venison is deep frozen no doubt, and my impression is that a good deal of it is eaten by the hunters themselves within a few days of killing it.

In Britain, some venison is deep frozen and some is canned. Apart from that, the amount that reaches the ordinary public is what remains after the hunters and their households, or the hotels that house them, the staff involved in the elaborate ritual of stalking the deer, and the hotels and restaurants who buy it directly from the landowners do not want. Venison that is left after those on the spot have had their fill is sent to the meat markets (Smithfield in London) and bought by those butchers with game licences. If more people knew how good and relatively cheap venison is it would be more easily available, for it is not only the expensive cuts that make delicious eating.

It is theoretically in season from June to the end of September for buck venison; does are available from October to December. In fact, there is very little venison in the shops before October, and what there is is almost certain to be deep frozen. The late autumn and winter are the best months, as the animals have had time to put on some fat, which improves the flavour enormously. But whatever the merits of the various types of deer, the best way of ensuring the success of the final dish is in its cooking.

Good-quality venison is dark red, finely grained, and its fat is white and firm. The best cuts are the haunch, the loin and the fillet, and these are most suitable for roasting, grilling, sautéing, and frying. The cheaper cuts can be used for stews and braising, but I am told that the standard of shooting has deteriorated, despite more sophisticated guns, and that the fore-quarters are so blasted by shot as to be almost unobtainable and often unusable. With the possible exception of the very best cut off the most tender animal, all venison is improved with marinating. However, because of the leanness of the meat, even the youngest needs plenty of fat to ensure its succulence.

For most of us who are unlikely to see the kill intact, the signs of the age of venison is more in the nature of an academic question. However, those with massive antlers with many tines, large and deeply cloven hooves, are probably better suited to decorative purposes, fur coats or rugs.

On a more practical basis, a large haunch is a reasonable indication that the animal from which it came is a mature one. Best of all, ask the butcher – if he is consistently wrong, go to another: there are some who specialize in knowing their game.

If given a piece of venison and it doesn't smell high by the time you get it, hang it smothered in ground ginger or pepper in a piece of muslin full of sprigs of thyme, rosemary and bay leaves or any other sweet-smelling herbs in a cool place. Make certain that the venison is absolutely dry before you put the spice on. The time for hanging depends on the weather; from seven days to a week or longer, in cold weather; less time in muggy warm weather, and make sure the place is well ventilated. Test the venison occasionally to see if it is ready by running a skewer through it nearest to the bone. If it smells at all high, it is ready to be cooked.

Before the cooking comes the marinating. If it is a whole haunch, a large quantity of the marinade will be needed to be effective. The basic marinade which is suggested is a guide to the proportions of wine to olive oil and flavourings. They can be adjusted to suit the size of the joint, or number of steaks or cutlets. Both the following marinades can be kept for some time in a refrigerator.

Average times for cooking venison are as follows: 15–20 minutes per pound for roasting and 2 hours minimum for slow cooking like braising or stewing for 2–3 pounds of meat in one piece.

Uncooked Marinade for Haunch of Venison

1 cup vinegar, 1 bottle dry white wine, ½ cup olive oil, 1 large sliced onion, 2 large sliced carrots, 4 sliced shallots, 3 sprigs parsley, 1 tsp. salt, 6 crushed peppercorns, 4 juniper berries, ¼ tsp. thyme.

Cooked Marinade

Chop 1 lb. carrots, 1 lb. onions, 1 head celery, let these sweat gently in 4 tbs. fat. Add 2 quarts vinegar, 1 quart red wine, plus 4 large sprigs of parsley, 3 crushed bay leaves, 1 tsp. thyme, 6 crushed peppercorns, 1 tbs. allspice, 1 tsp. salt. Boil mixture for ½ hour and cool before using.

Roast Haunch of Venison

2–2½ lb. haunch of venison, 6 oz. bacon fat or salt pork cut into strips, 4 oz. beef dripping or butter, salt, pepper.

MARINADE

4 tbs. oil, 1 glass red wine vinegar, 1 large onion, 1 clove garlic, bouquet garni.

Lard the haunch with the strips of fat and marinade for 8–12 hours. Remove the venison from the marinade, wipe it dry, spread with butter, cook in a medium-hot oven for about 2 hours. Baste with 3 oz. of the butter or fat, and a little of the marinade. Make a sauce as described for Fillet of Venison. Serve with red-currant jelly or apple purée, salad, and jacket or roast potatoes.

A traditional way, still most effective, of roasting haunch or saddle of venison which prevents the meat drying. If in doubt about the age of the venison, marinate it overnight before cooking in either marinade suggested above. If the haunch is from a young animal, there is no need to marinate it. In any case, you must remove the membrane and sinews. This is an excellent dish for a dinner party of eight people, but like any meal with a roast, your guests may have to wait a while until it is quite ready. Personally, I have never found any problem in guests waiting between courses. However, be prepared to provide enough wine to keep the atmosphere convivial – alternatively, avoid guests who get restive between courses, when you serve meals of this sort.

Roast Venison in Pastry Case

3 lb. flour, water, 1¼ lb. chopped suet, salt, ¼ lb. butter, 12 tbs. red-currant/cranberry jelly, cooking foil, 1 pt meat stock.

For a saddle or haunch, use 3 lb. flour and mix it with water to a stiff dough and roll out to ½ inch thickness. Alternatively, a suet pastry (see p. 164) can be used, which will of course be quite delicious to eat. Cover the entire joint with foil, which is much easier to handle than the greaseproof paper formerly used. Then roll the pastry round the foil, so that the joint is completely sealed in, then another covering of foil to complete the process. A large haunch or saddle should be cooked allowing 25 minutes to the pound, in a warm oven (no. 4). It will take about 4 hours to cook. Fifteen minutes before it is ready take off the foil and pastry covering and dust the meat with flour and salt, and baste with melted butter. Return the joint to the oven to brown. Serve with plenty of cranberry or red-currant jelly, gravy made with the pan juices and 1 pint of meat stock.

The suet crust will be good enough to eat, so no potatoes are necessary. Above all, see that all the plates and dishes are really hot.

Personally, I like to carve joints on a spiked wooden carving board with runnels for catching the juices; lay the fairly thickly cut slices on a fire-proof dish kept hot on an asbestos mat on the stove. A very little of the gravy thinned with some red wine stops the carved slices from getting dry or overcooking appreciably.

Grilled Venison Steaks

4 venison steaks from the haunch, salt, pepper, 2 large cooking apples, 2 oz. butter.

MARINADE
2 tbs. olive oil, 1 wine glass cider, 6 crushed peppercorns, salt.

Marinate the steaks in the oil, cider, peppercorns and salt for three hours. Make a purée with the apples. Drain and dry the steaks, brush with melted butter and grill for 10–15 minutes under a moderately hot grill, turning the steaks twice during cooking. Baste often with the remains of the butter. Reduce the marinade by half and dilute the cooking juices. Add more seasoning if necessary. Pour over the steaks and serve with the apple purée; a very thick purée of plums or a mixture of grated horseradish and beetroot mixed with wine vinegar is equally good. Sauté potatoes go well with this dish.

Fillet of Venison

2 lb. fillet of venison, 2 egg yolks, 1 tbs. French mustard.

MARINADE
2 glasses red wine, 2 tbs. olive oil, 4 crushed peppercorns, bouquet garni, 4 crushed juniper berries, 2 oz. butter, salt, pepper.

Marinate the fillet for 24 hours in the red wine, oil etc. Drain and dry. Roast in oven (no. 5) for about 45–50 minutes basting frequently with melted butter and half the strained marinade. When the fillet is almost cooked reduce the remainder of the marinade and add it to the gravy. Beat the egg yolks and mix with the mustard. Add this mixture very gradually to the gravy to thicken it. Serve with baked jacket potatoes and green salad.

Sautéed Venison Steaks

2 lb. haunch of venison cut in thin slices, 1 glass wine vinegar, 1 glass red wine, 1 chopped shallot, bouquet garni, 1 onion, cloves, cinnamon, 4 oz. butter, 1 small glass brandy, 1 cup stock, 1 tbs. flour, salt, pepper.

Make a cooked marinade with the wine, vinegar, an onion, bouquet garni and chopped shallot, allowing these to simmer for about 15 minutes. When cool pour the marinade over the venison and allow to stand for an hour or two. Then drain and dry the meat. Cook the fillets for 10–15 minutes in very hot butter in a shallow pan. Then put them in a fire-proof serving dish. Add the marinade, brandy, stock and a little beurre manié. Reduce the sauce and cook the venison in it for another 5 minutes or so. Serve with chestnut purée (see p. 161) and red-currant or rowan jelly.

Venison Cutlets with Chestnuts

4 large or 8 small venison cutlets, 3 tbs. olive oil, 2 oz. butter, salt and pepper, 1 lb. shelled chestnuts, ¼ pt cream, red-currant jelly, 1 small glass red wine.

MARINADE

1 glass red wine, pepper, 2–3 bay leaves.

Marinate the cutlets for 2–3 hours before cooking. Boil the chestnuts and make a purée with cream. Dry and season and then sauté the cutlets quickly in the hot oil and butter for about 7 minutes or more either side. Pour excess fat from the pan, add 2 tbs. red-currant jelly, and a small glass of red wine. Serve the cutlets with the sauce, chestnut purée and a crisp green salad.

Saddle or Haunch of Venison with Sour Cream

3 lb. saddle or haunch of venison in one piece, 2 cloves garlic, 1 tbs. freshly ground black pepper, 1 lb. diced bacon fat, 4 oz. butter, ½ pt sour cream, ¾ lb. mushrooms, 2 dill-pickled cucumbers, ¼ tsp. dill, salt, pepper.

MARINADE
See p. 144.

Remove all large pieces of membrane from saddle or haunch. Marinate the venison for 3 days before cooking. Dry it thoroughly and push in slivers of cloves of garlic here and there, and pepper the meat well on all sides. Melt the bacon fat in the butter, and when it is ready pour it all over the meat in the roasting pan. Add 4 tbs.

of the marinade to this fat, and baste the venison frequently with the mixture during the first 45 minutes of roasting. During the next 15 minutes start basting with half the quantity (¼ pt) of sour cream with the dill added. While the meat is cooking, clean the mushrooms and chop the cucumbers finely. Place the mushrooms in the roasting pan, where they will cook during the last 10 minutes of the venison's roasting time. Remove the venison, which should not be dried out nor rare (try it with a very fine skewer if you are in doubt) and put it on a well-heated fire-proof serving dish and keep it hot. Put the roasting pan on top of the stove, add the remainder of the sour cream and stir it well with the pan juices and all the crusty bits. Add the chopped cucumber and heat through for 5 minutes, stirring all the time. Serve with rice or noodles.

Venison with Cherries

2 lb. loin or haunch of venison in one piece, 3 oz. butter, 1 large onion sliced, 1 tbs. flour, 1 liqueur glass kirsch, 2 cups preserved cherries preferably black, zest of lemon, salt, pepper.

MARINADE

Juice of 3 lemons, 2 tbs. oil, 1 tsp. crushed coriander, 1 crushed bay leaf, 3 sprigs thyme, 2 cloves garlic.

Marinate the venison for 6–8 hours. Drain, dry and brown the meat in the butter in a heavy fire-proof pan with the sliced onions. Flame the venison with the kirsch, sprinkle on the flour and pour on the strained marinade and the red wine. Simmer on top of the stove for 2½ hours. Cut the zest of one lemon into very fine slivers. Ten minutes before serving add the cherries, and if the sauce is too thin add a knob of beurre manié. Carve into thick slices and serve on a very hot dish surrounded by the cherries. Sprinkle the zest of lemon onto the venison. Potatoes, rice or croûtons go well with this dish.

Venison Cutlets Paprika

4 large or 8 small cutlets, salt, 2 tbs. paprika, 4 oz. butter, 1 glass Madeira, ½ pt cream, juice of ½ lemon.

MARINADE
See p. 144.

If the cutlets are from an elderly piece of venison, marinate for 3 hours. If young, they should not need marinating. Sprinkle the cutlets with paprika and salt and sauté them for 15 minutes in butter. Add 1 small glass of Madeira to the pan juices, mix well then pour in the cream. Heat almost to boiling, adding a little lemon juice. Pour mixture over the cutlets. Serve chestnut purée separately.

Breaded Venison Chops

8 loin chops of very young venison, 2 cups fine white breadcrumbs, 2 beaten eggs, 2 tsp. coarsely ground black pepper, salt, 4 crushed juniper berries, 4 oz. butter, 1 tbs. olive oil, handful chopped parsley.

Wipe off any moisture from the chops. Dip each chop in the egg. Add the juniper berries and salt and pepper to the breadcrumbs and then dip the chops into them. Then dip into the egg a second time. Heat the butter and oil until it is just beginning to give off a blue haze in a large frying-pan or sauteuse, big enough to hold all the meat. Brown the chops lightly on a moderately hot flame and put them in the oven (no. 3) for 45–60 minutes, depending on the thickness of the chops. Turn twice during cooking so that the batter is evenly cooked both sides. Sprinkle with fresh parsley and serve with a purée of chestnuts, a segment of lemon and red-currant or cranberry jelly.

The double-coating of breadcrumbs and egg prevents the venison from drying out during cooking and the batter has a lovely crisp consistency.

Venison Chops with Sour Cream à la Russe

4 venison chops from the loin, 2–3 oz. butter, ¼ pt sour cream, salt, pepper.

Marinate the chops in uncooked marinade (see p. 144) for 24 hours, turning occasionally. Remove and wipe dry and season with pepper and a little salt. Sauté in the butter on a moderately hot fire for about 7 minutes a side. Remove the chops from the pan and keep hot on a serving dish. Add ½ cup strained marinade to the pan and blend well with cooking juices. Bring to the boil, then stir in sour cream, heat again but do not boil. Adjust seasoning. Serve the sauce separately with the chops. Rice or buckwheat (see p. 160) goes well with this dish.

Venison Fillets

2½–3 lb. tender young venison cut into 8 ¼-inch slices, 4 oz. butter, ½ pt meat stock, 1 clove garlic, ¼ tsp. cinnamon, grated rind of 1 lemon, 1 glass dry red wine, 6 slices white bread for croûtons, salt, pepper.

Flatten 4 ¼-inch thick slices of tender venison and cut them into pieces about 3 inches long and 1½ inches wide. Make a sauce with a brown roux (see p. 24) from the flour and 1 oz. of butter and the stock. Add the crushed clove of garlic, the cinnamon, grated lemon rind and red wine, pepper and salt. While the sauce is simmering, fry the slices of venison in the rest of the butter in another pan, for 5 minutes either side. Put them on a heated dish and pour the thickened sauce over them. Serve on croûtons, with gooseberry or any red berry preserve.

For the less tender cuts of venison.

Casserole of Venison with Sauerkraut

2½ lb. stewing venison, 2 tbs. flour, ¼ lb. diced bacon, ½ pt beer, 2 large sliced onions, 4 diced carrots, 2 sliced bratwurst (German sausage), 1 lb. sauerkraut, 2 tsp. capers, salt, pepper.

MARINADE

1 tbs. olive oil, 4 tbs. beer, 1 crushed clove garlic.

Cover the venison with the marinade and allow it to stand, in an earthenware dish, for 3 hours, turning occasionally. Dry the venison, cut into 2-inch cubes, sprinkle with flour, season, and brown with the bacon. Add the vegetables and the marinade. Simmer with the lid on for 1½ hours. Drain the sauerkraut, add the bratwurst and then all the venison and vegetables. Heat these together for 10 minutes with the capers. Serve with noodles or dumplings.

Stewed Venison

2 lb. venison, 2 sliced onions, 2 sliced carrots, 1 clove garlic, bouquet garni, 2 tbs. flour, stick of celery, 6 oz. mild bacon in one piece, pepper, salt.

MARINADE

2 glasses vermouth, ½ glass wine vinegar, 3 cloves garlic, 1 bay leaf.

Cut the venison into 2-inch cubes and marinate them overnight. Drain the venison. Brown the bacon and onions in a heat-proof dish just large enough for all the ingredients. When enough fat has melted from the bacon, sauté the meat for about 10 minutes. Sprinkle on the flour, and brown. Add the strained marinade, the bouquet, the garlic and the sliced carrots. Season with salt and pepper and cover tightly. Cook for 2 hours in a low oven (no. 2). If the lid does not fit closely enough, put a layer of foil underneath it. Serve with a purée of mashed potatoes or turnips. The vermouth adds a very pleasant aromatic flavour, and is a change from the more usual red wine marinade.

Stewed Breast of Venison

3 lb. breast of venison.

MARINADE

1 sliced onion, 1 tbs. allspice, bay leaf, parsley, salt, ½ bottle red wine vinegar.

Marinate for 24 hours. Cook the meat in the marinade in a heavy pan, bringing it to the boil first and then simmering, tightly covered, for about 3 hours. Before serving, thicken the liquid with beurre manié. Potatoes, parsnips and other root vegetables added to the casserole about 30 minutes before serving makes a delicious garnish. Alternatively, this dish can be served with dumplings.

Venison Stroganoff

2 lb. of thin venison slices from the haunch, 4 oz. butter, 2 lb.

Spanish onions sliced, 1 lb. mushrooms, 1 pt sour cream, 1 tbs. French mustard, salt, pepper, 1 tsp. fresh chopped tarragon or parsley.

MARINADE

1 glass white wine, 2 tbs. oil and juice of 1 lemon.

Marinate the venison steaks for 2 hours. Dry, and cut into strips ¼-inch wide and 2 inches long. Sauté the onions in 2 oz. butter, but do not let them brown. Remove and keep warm in a shallow heat-proof dish, either in the oven or on top of the stove. Sauté the mushrooms and place them together with the onions. Reduce the marinade and add it to the onions and mushrooms. In the remaining 2 oz. butter, fry the venison strips for about 2–3 minutes. Reheat the mushrooms and onions on top of the stove and add the sour cream and the French mustard. Mix together so that all the sauce gets evenly distributed. Add the fried venison to this mixture, stir well, and add lots of black pepper, and salt to taste and sprinkle with the herbs. Serve on mashed potatoes, rice or noodles.

Venison Pie

3 lb. neck or breast of venison, 2 onions, 2 carrots, 1 clove garlic, 1 glass sherry, madeira or port, bouquet garni with two bay leaves, 1 tsp. oregano, ½ lb. mushrooms, 1 oz. butter, salt, pepper.

PASTRY

¼ lb. suet or butter, ½ lb. flour, 1 tbs. water, salt.

Chop the meat and boil it quite slowly, for 2 hours, in water with the clove garlic, onions, carrots, salt and pepper in a covered pan. Strain off the broth (keep this for game soups) and when the meat is cool, remove it from the bones. Add a glass of sherry, port or Madeira, a cup of the stock, a bouquet garni with 2 bay leaves and a pinch of oregano. Simmer for another 10 minutes. When this cools, put the meat and gravy in a pie dish with ½ lb. mushrooms sautéed in butter. Cover with pastry, and cook for 25 minutes in a moderate oven.

Raised Game Pie – Venison

A raised game pie can be made with any game meat and also a mixture of game meats. In practice, those game which will be most readily available in large quantities will be venison, hare and rabbit. Clearly a game pie which contains hare or venison will be more strongly flavoured than one with larger quantities of rabbit. Alternatively, more or less veal or pork, ham or tongue can be added as well as hard-boiled eggs, truffles, pistachios.

Bear

Unfortunately, my own experience of eating bear is limited. In this case, I have to take on trust the opinions of my friends who have eaten it as I have learnt not to be incredulous about any food. After I discovered what I thought to be delicious sucking pig was in fact a badger, I decided there and then to 'suspend my disbelief'.

It seems reasonable that since the bear's diet (anyway those roaming in the wilds) includes such delicious things as berries, honey and fruit, its flesh should be equally delectable. But it is a muscular beast, and to make it edible it must be marinated for some time before cooking. No doubt, the smoked hams which Fortnum and Mason sold at one time were given very careful preparatory treatment. In Russia where bear ham is said to be common, the hams are cured like pork – it is eaten raw like the more commonplace Jambon de Bayonne or Parma Ham. There are stories about bears' paws being a great delicacy in China in pre-Confucian times. I rate these with the tales of my friend brought up in Tienstin, who claims that his father, having fled the Bolshevik revolution, was regaled with a fabulous meal on his way to Harbin – the *pièce de résistance* being monkeys' brains.

In any case, it is as well to know what to do with it, should you be given a haunch, loin or part of a bear. A small dinner party of bear meat seems to me a contradiction in terms – either it has to be a fairly large party or not at all. And as you will have to marinate the meat for five days, there will be plenty of time for preparation!

Cooked Marinade
appropriate to all the recipes for Bear

2 pts dry white wine, 2 sliced onions, 2 sliced carrots, 1 whole head of coarsely chopped celery, chopped shallots, 2 crushed cloves of garlic, 3 bay leaves, 12 crushed peppercorns, 4 crushed juniper berries, 1 tbs. fresh or ½ tsp. dried tarragon, 1 tbs. salt.

To prepare the marinade, bring all the ingredients to the boil 3 or 4 times, then let it cool.

Roast Loin of Bear

6 lb. piece of loin of bear, 6 oz. strips of pork for larding, ½ pt cream.

Lard the loin and place in an earthenware dish, so that the loin just fits into it, allowing the marinade to cover it completely. Leave for five days at least. The cooking will take about 3 hours in all.

Dry the meat when taken out of the marinade, and strain off the vegetables from it. Place the vegetables at the bottom of the roasting pan and the meat on top of that. In a hot oven (no. 8) roast for 15 minutes. Then turn the oven down to no. 4 and roast for another 2 hours, basting often with the pan juices. When the meat is tender put it on a warm fire-proof serving dish and keep it at the bottom of the oven at the lowest possible heat. To make the sauce, pour a cup of the marinade into the roasting pan on top of the stove, scrape off all the bits sticking to the pan, stir well and heat it gently for ¼ hour. Add the cream and bring it to the boil very slowly. Pour the sauce from the pan through the sieve pressing it through with a wooden spoon, so that as much of the vegetables gets pushed through as possible. Half this sauce should cover the bear meat, and the rest should be served separately. Garnish with watercress and any tart red berry preserve, as well as croûtons. Personally, I feel that it would be more poetic with buckwheat (see p. 160) a cereal I associate with Russia. This dish is enough for 12 people.

A less spectacular meal can be made with steaks from the loin, but

I still think that meat one eats as infrequently as bear deserves a festive occasion.

Bear Steaks

8 6–8 oz. slices of loin of bear, not less than ½ inch thick, 2 cloves garlic, 3 oz. butter, 2 tbs. chopped chives, 1 dessertspoon French or German mustard, 2 large Spanish onions finely chopped, 3 tbs. tomato purée, 2 tsp. lemon juice, salt, black pepper coarsely ground, 2 tsp. paprika, ½ lb. mushrooms, 2 tbs. chopped parsley.

Marinate the bear steaks in the cooked marinade described on p. 154, for a minimum of 24 hours. Heat the grill so that it is really glowing before you start cooking the steaks. Drain and dry the steaks and sprinkle coarsely ground pepper on them. Sear the steaks briefly on both sides under the grill, turn down the heat and cook slowly for about 7 minutes either side, basting frequently with one ounce of the melted butter. Turn the steaks at least twice during cooking. Meanwhile, place the remaining butter in a shallow fire-proof dish large enough for all the steaks to lie flat in. Take all the ingredients that remain, i.e. the chopped vegetables, spices and seasoning, and mash them evenly with the butter. Keep this warm. When the bear steaks are ready, place them on the butter mixture and leave them in the oven. Grill the mushrooms in the melted fat from the steaks, and cover the steaks with the mushrooms, and sprinkle with parsley before serving. Serve with sauté potatoes. The highly flavoured butter with the mild chopped Spanish onions makes a pleasant change from maître d'hôtel butter.

For the lesser cuts of bear than loin or haunch, marinating and extremely slow cooking can produce a very good ragoût.

Stewed Bear in Wine

2 lb. of lean bear meat cut up in 2-inch cubes, 2 tbs. flour, ¼ lb. diced fat salt pork, 1 oz. butter, 2 glasses red wine, 2 cloves garlic, 24 button onions, sliced carrots, salt, pepper.

Marinate the meat in the cooked marinade (see p. 154) but reduce the quantities appropriately for the lesser quantity of meat, and allow it to stand for 12 hours. Drain the meat dry and sprinkle with flour. In a heavy sauteuse melt the diced fat pork until all the fat has run out, then take out the remaining pieces. Add the butter to the pork fat and brown the meat on a brisk heat all over. Pour in the red wine and the strained marinade, and add the two crushed cloves of garlic. Cover tightly and simmer for four hours. If the meat appears to be getting dry add a little more wine. During the long cooking of the meat, peel and glaze the onions and sliced carrots (see p. 162). Add these to the stew 15 minutes before serving. Adjust the seasoning and serve with potato dumplings.

Boar

If wild boar exist in British forests, it is because they have escaped from a zoo; in central Europe, France and in certain States of North America they are still hunted and considered great delicacies. The young boar, up to the age of six months, is known in France as marcassin, and in the winter months certain restaurants in Paris and elsewhere keep it for special customers. The flavour is similar to pork only more so, and being lean, does not have the unctuousness of pork.

All parts of the young boar are very good eating but are much improved by marinating; the only culinary use for an old boar is the contribution which the head makes to certain ceremonial occasions. In general, wild boar can be cooked in a variety of ways suitable for either venison or pork as long as it is kept well basted when roast or moist in slow cooking.

Allow about 20 minutes per pound when roasting and two hours for slow cooking, and about half a pound of uncooked meat for each serving.

Recipes

A whole haunch or saddle of wild boar deserves a special feast and extravagant Wagnerian portions of food and drink.

Roast Haunch or Saddle of Wild Boar

4 lb. leg or saddle of young boar, 6 strips of salt pork, 6 oz. butter, 1 glass brandy, salt, pepper.

MARINADE

1 bottle red wine, 6 crushed juniper berries, 2 sliced onions, 1 clove garlic, 1 sliced carrot, 1 bay leaf, salt and pepper.

Marinate the haunch for 8 hours. Drain, dry and lard it with the strips of pork fat. Spread butter liberally all over the haunch and cook it in a hot oven (no. 7) for 10 minutes. Turn down the oven to no. 5 and baste frequently with melted butter and some of the marinade, for another hour. Make a sauce with the pan juices, a glass of burnt brandy and enough of the marinade to absorb all the crusty bits sticking to the pan, while the haunch is kept hot on a fire-proof dish. Serve with roast potatoes, red cabbage and apple purée.

Boiled Shoulder of Wild Boar

2–4 lb. shoulder of wild boar, salt, pepper, 1 oz. butter, 1 tbs. flour, 1 tbs. mustard, ½ pt cream, 1 tsp. capers.

MARINADE

2 glasses white wine, 1 glass wine vinegar, 2 sliced onions, 2 sliced carrots, 4 crushed peppercorns, ½ tsp. dill, salt.

Marinate for 4 hours. Drain and put the meat in a saucepan and cover it halfway with cold water. Add half the marinade, some salt and pepper and poach for 2 hours. Take the tender meat out and keep it hot. Make a roux with the butter and flour, add the remains of the marinade liquid and thicken. Mix the mustard into the cream, add the capers and stir into sauce. Serve boar with noodles and hand the sauce separately.

Cutlets of Wild Boar

4–8 cutlets, 2 sliced onions, 3 oz. butter, ¼ pt sour cream.

MARINADE

2 glasses red wine, bay leaf, 4 crushed juniper berries, 1 clove garlic, salt, pepper.

Marinate the cutlets overnight. Drain, dry and brown them in a shallow fire-proof pan in the butter, add the sliced onion. Add half the marinade, cover and cook in a moderate oven for 30 minutes. If the meat shows any signs of drying out, add more of the marinade. When the cutlets are tender, put them into a serving dish in the oven. Add the sour cream to the juices in the pan, season with salt and a good sprinkling of black pepper. Serve the cutlets with grilled mushrooms, tomatoes and sauté potatoes, and the sauce, handed separately.

Buffalo

If you think this sounds improbable, a whole fillet of buffalo only weighs 3 pounds. However, I now give you – Buffalo fillet!

Buffalo Fillet

1 fillet of buffalo, 4 oz. butter, ½ sliced onion, 1 tbs. chopped parsley, large pinch marjoram, tarragon and mace, 1 glass red wine, ¼ pt rich stock, 2 tbs. red-currant jelly, salt and pepper.

MARINADE

2 glasses port, 3 tbs. mushroom ketchup, 1 tbs. brown sugar, ¼ cup espagnole sauce, ¾ glass wine vinegar, ½ tsp. salt, pinch of cayenne pepper, 2 bay leaves, 1 sliced onion, 1 sliced carrot, 2 cloves crushed garlic, 8 crushed peppercorns, ¼ tsp. thyme.

Mix all the marinade ingredients and warm in a double-boiler for 30 minutes. Before marinating the fillet, trim off any fat and tie with fine string so that it will keep its shape when cooking. Having done that, marinate the fillet in (this time) the warm marinade and leave it for 48 hours. Turn it over every so often. When it is ready to cook, wipe the fillet dry. In a large shallow pan sear the fillet in the butter. Reduce the heat, add the half onion, chopped parsley, marjoram, tarragon, and mace, and season with pepper and salt. Cover the fillet with foil and cook in a low oven (no. 3) for 45 minutes, basting at least every 10 minutes with melted butter and hot water in the roasting pan, which will prevent the fillet drying out. While the fillet is cooking, strain half a glass of marinade into a small saucepan and reduce it, then add the stock. Make the final sauce by adding a glass of red wine to the butter in the roasting pan, pepper and salt and 2 tablespoons of red-currant jelly to the reduced marinade and stock. Bring to the boil. Carve the fillet or as much as you want for a first helping and strain the sauce over the slices. Serve with jacket potatoes.

Squirrel

Wild squirrels are considered delicious game food in America but are not (as far as we know) eaten in Britain. Only an old squirrel should need marinating, young ones can be cooked like rabbit or chicken.

Squirrel Stew

2 young squirrels, 6 onions, 6 tomatoes, 3 sweet peppers, thyme, 1 tbs. flour, 2 oz. or 4 tbs. butter or dripping, 1½ pts water.

Cut the squirrels into two pieces and dredge with flour. Brown in a shallow pan with the sliced onion. Meanwhile, boil the water and add the tomatoes and peppers coarsely chopped to it, in either a heavy stew-pan or earthenware casserole, into which you have placed the squirrels and onions. Cover the pan closely and simmer for 1 hour. Add 1 lb. peas or shelled broad beans, and cook until the vegetables are tender. If the gravy needs thickening, add 1 tablespoon of beurre manié.

ACCOMPANIMENTS

Apple Purée

1 lb. cooking apples cored and peeled, sugar (if necessary).

Put the sliced apples in a covered pan and simmer very gently – no water is necessary if they are cooked slowly. When they are soft beat them until they are quite smooth. Evaporate the liquid until the purée is nice and thick.

Buckwheat for game

This cereal, mostly eaten in Russia and central Europe, has a nutty flavour quite unlike rice, semolina, barley or other better known cereals.

Heat ½ lb. of buckwheat in a pan until it is slightly browned. Put it into a fireproof dish, season with salt and pepper, add 2 oz. butter and boiling water to cover. Cook in a slow oven for about 2–2½ hours. It should have a thin crust on top but the grains should be separate underneath. Alternatively, it can be cooked in a double boiler with the same mixture of butter and water. Do not brown it beforehand. Cook for 2–2½ hours on a low heat.

To make buckwheat cakes add 2 oz. butter to the buckwheat made in the double boiler. Press it flat on a large dish with a plate on top of it to a thickness of ½ inch. Cut it into shapes with a pastry cutter or the rim of a glass. These can be browned in clarified butter. Buckwheat keeps well in a refrigerator and can be prepared in advance.

Buttered and Fried Breadcrumbs

Put a cupful of breadcrumbs into 1 oz. melted butter in a pan, and stir over a very low heat until all the butter is absorbed without browning the breadcrumbs; to fry, let them brown evenly.

Dry them on kitchen paper. They will keep for a week stored in an airtight jar.

Celery or Celeriac Purée

1 good thick bunch of celery, or 1 lb. celeriac, salt, pepper, 1 oz. butter, 3 tbs. cream.

Cook the chunks of celery or celeriac in boiling salted water, over a low heat. Drain; mash it evenly, add more seasoning, the butter and the cream and reheat before serving.

Chestnut Purée

This can be made with dried chestnuts already peeled or whole chestnuts. For the peeled, dried chestnuts, wash them in a colander, then soak in water overnight. For whole chestnuts, roast or boil and remove shell but do not soak before cooking with the milk. Put them with the remaining water into a saucepan and add enough milk to cover. When they are quite soft make a purée with a moulinette (see p. 29) or in a blender, add 2 oz. butter, salt and pepper, and 2 tablespoons cream.

Forcemeat Dumplings

Instead of stuffing forcemeat into the body of the bird or animal, it can be rolled into little balls and cooked separately to accompany a dish. These little dumplings are especially good with casseroled dishes. This one is made with hare offal but can be adapted to suit any game. Hare's liver, kidneys and heart, 1 cup breadcrumbs, 1 tbs. chopped parsley, 1 oz. butter or shredded suet, salt, pepper, 1 large onion finely chopped, 2 beaten eggs, flour. Blanch the hare offal in salted water, drain and mince finely (or chop). Mix with the breadcrumbs, fat, onion and parsley, salt and pepper. Roll into little balls and flour lightly. Poach in boiling salted water or in stock.

Forcemeat Stuffing for Game

½ lb. liver (of game), ¼ lb. belly of pork (pork fat), ½ lb. young rabbit meat, 1 oz. foie gras, 2 tbs. butter, 3 egg yolks, 2 tbs. espagnole sauce, seasoning and ½ cup Madeira.

Chop or mince the liver, pork and rabbit meat and blend with the foie gras and butter. Bind with the egg yolks and sauce, season and add the Madeira.

Game Chips

These are thicker than the commercially sold crisps. The easiest way to cut them is with an electric mincer which has a gadget for slicing vegetables. The next best thing is a mandolin (see p. 29); deft people can cut them up incredibly quickly with a sharp knife. Let the potato slices stand in cold water for a few minutes, then drain and dry completely. Put the chips into a frying basket and lower into boiling oil. When they are still only a light brown, remove them from the fat. Reheat the fat till it is smoking hot, lower the potatoes in, cook for three minutes; drain and dry.

Game Jelly (See Fish Jelly, p. 85)

Proportions are: 2½ lb. game carcasses and trimmings, just browned in the oven, aromatic vegetables, 12 juniper berries and bouquet garni.

Glazed Carrots, Onions etc.

1 lb young carrots, 1 oz butter, 2 tsp. caster sugar, 2 cups stock.

Put the carrots into a small saucepan with the other ingredients and simmer slowly without a lid for ½ hour or longer depending on their size.

Gravy for Game

½ pt game stock made from the giblets and trimmings, 1 oz. flour, salt, pepper, juice of ½ lemon, small glass of sherry or red wine.

Make a brown roux (see p. 24) with the flour and butter, season and add the stock gradually. Cook on a moderate heat while stirring to keep the gravy smooth, add the sherry or wine and serve hot.

Pastry for a Game Pâté

10 oz. flour, 7 oz. unsalted butter, 2 eggs, pinch salt, 3 tbs. water.

Sift 10 oz. flour into a bowl. Separate egg yolks from white and beat them gently into the softened butter. When they are thoroughly mixed add the water and then the flour very gradually to avoid making the dough lumpy. Allow the dough to chill before rolling out. When the mould is filled and the pastry lid in place, it can be glazed by brushing with some egg yolk.

Polenta

This is made from yellow maize flour and eaten in many parts of Italy.

½ lb. maize flour, 1½ oz. butter, 1 pt water, salt, pepper.

Stir the flour into a large saucepan of salted boiling water. When it thickens, simmer for ½ hour stirring constantly until it is all quite smooth. Add the butter and season with more salt and pepper. If allowed to cool, it can be cut into pieces and fried or reheated in the oven with a little melted butter.

Pommes Dauphine

2 lb. potatoes, salt, pepper, 1 cup grated parmesan or gruyère cheese; for those who like garlic, the surface of the dish can be smeared with a cut clove of garlic first.

Slice the potatoes fairly thinly, season with pepper and salt. Butter an earthenware dish; lay the potato slices in the dish so that they overlap round the sides, fill up with layers of potato sprinkled with grated cheese; pour over the rest of the butter melted. Cook in a medium oven but raise the temperature 5 minutes before serving to brown the top.

For a change, add 2 beaten eggs and a tablespoon of cream about 10 minutes before the potatoes are cooked. Make sure all the liquid is absorbed before serving.

Pommes Anna

These are thinly sliced potatoes washed to remove some of the starch surplus, dried and then sautéed in butter. When they have absorbed the butter, but before browning, press them down with a fork so that they form a kind of flat cake. Brown under a grill on one side and turn them over and repeat the process. Slide them out of the pan onto a heated serving dish.

Pommes Lyonnaise

1 lb. potatoes, 2 oz. butter, 1 onion.

Mix some very thinly sliced fried onion with well-browned sautéed potatoes.

Ratatouille

2 sliced Spanish (or other mild) onions, 2 sliced sweet peppers (pimento), 2 sliced aubergines, 4 quartered tomatoes, 2 garlic cloves, olive oil, salt, pepper.

Sauté the onions first in the moderately hot oil; after 10 minutes add the peppers and aubergines and 10 minutes later the tomatoes and garlic. Season with salt and pepper. Simmer slowly for 45 minutes leaving the pan uncovered for 15 minutes before serving, to thicken mixture a little.

Suet Crust for Pigeon, Grouse and other Puddings

3 oz. shredded suet to 6 oz. of flour, or 3 oz. flour and 3 oz. fresh white breadcrumbs (for 1½ pt pudding basin).

Mix together with 1 tsp. baking powder and a pinch of salt. Add enough water to make a firm paste, which should leave the mixing bowl quite clean. Roll out as soon as possible to about ½ inch thick. Use fresh beef suet preferably and chop it yourself. Line the pudding basin and leave enough for the lid.

SAUCES

Aspic Jelly made with gelatine, for Fish or Game

1 pt concentrated fish stock or game stock, 1 oz. gelatine, 2 beaten egg whites, 2 crushed egg shells, 3 tbs. white wine (use ¼ less stock for diced aspic jelly).

Dissolve the gelatine in 2 tablespoons of warmed stock and add it to the rest of the stock in a large pan. Add the whisked egg whites and the shells, and stir while bringing the liquid to the boil. Reduce the heat and simmer for 3 minutes. Allow to stand for 15 minutes and then strain it through a muslin-covered conical strainer. Add salt and pepper if necessary and the wine. Let it cool. If it is to be spooned over the food use the aspic just before it sets. If the jelly is going to be diced as part of the decoration, then it must set hard.

Apricot Sauce for all Game

½ lb. dried apricots soaked until soft, juice of ½ lemon, 1 tsp. grated orange peel, ½ wine glass of sherry, sugar to taste, pinch of ground ginger, 1 tbs. brandy.

Cook the apricots in a saucepan with enough water just to cover them, including the remains of the water they were soaked in. When they are soft rub them through a sieve or purée in an electric blender (blenders always bleach the contents, so they will not be such a deep colour) with the lemon juice and the sherry. Add the sugar and ground ginger and the brandy just before serving. Equally good hot or cold.

Béarnaise Sauce

This can be made by adding tarragon and chervil to hollandaise sauce (see p. 170).

4 oz. butter, 3 egg yolks, 4 tbs. vinegar, 2 tbs. tarragon vinegar, 2 shallots chopped, pepper, salt, lemon juice, 3 or 4 leaves fresh tarragon, and a sprig of chervil. The tarragon is the more characteristic flavour in this sauce.

Béchamel Sauce

1 oz. butter, 1 tbs. (½ oz.) flour, 1 pt hot milk, pepper, salt, optional flavourings include minced onion, one half to these quantities of the other ingredients. The addition of chopped veal or ham, rich stock or beaten egg yolk can be used to vary the basic sauce.

Melt the butter in a thick saucepan or double boiler, stir in the flour and cook gently without browning for 3–5 minutes. Add the heated milk little by little, stirring all the time to prevent the mixture getting lumpy. When all the sauce begins to thicken and bubble add any extra seasoning, and let it simmer for 10 minutes gently. Strain through a fine sieve; cover with melted butter to prevent a skin forming, if it is to be kept for later use.

Beurre Blanc

1 glass white wine vinegar, 1 chopped shallot, 8 oz. softened butter, freshly ground black pepper.

Add the chopped shallot to the wine vinegar and reduce it almost to nothing. Move the saucepan from the fire and add the 8 oz. butter, stirring all the time. Add a pinch of freshly ground black pepper.

Brown Chaud-froid Sauce

1 tsp. gelatine, dissolved in 1 cup water, 1 pt brown sauce, ½ pt stock, ½ glass sherry or Madeira.

Boil the brown (espagnole, see p. 169) sauce with the stock and remove the scum. Take the saucepan off the heat and dissolve the gelatine in it. Add the sherry or Madeira and strain.

Sauce Bigarade
Particularly good with wild duck.

The zest (see p. 17) of 2 bitter oranges, cut into thin strips, 1 pt espagnole sauce, juice of 1 orange, 1 tsp. lemon juice, salt, pepper.

Put the strips of orange into a small pan, covered with cold water and bring it gently to the boil. Drain off the water and add the espagnole sauce; simmer gently until the zest of orange is soft. Add the juice of both oranges and lemon and season to taste. A spoonful of sherry or Madeira may be added as variations as well as redcurrant or other tart jelly.

Bread Sauce
For partridge, pheasant, rabbit and hare.

1 onion stuck with 2 cloves, 1 pt milk, salt, 4 peppercorns, ½ oz. butter, ¾ cup fine white breadcrumbs, pinch grated nutmeg.

Put the onion into the milk in a small saucepan and bring it to the boil. Turn off the heat and let the contents stand for about ½ hour so that the onion flavour exudes into the milk. Spoon out the peppercorns, add all the other ingredients and cook gently for ¼ hour. Remove onion before serving.

Sauce Catalan
4 cloves garlic, 1 lb. tomatoes, 2 tbs. olive oil, 1 tsp. sugar, 11 slices orange.

Put 4 cloves of garlic and 1 lb. of tomatoes into a sauteuse with 2 tablespoons of olive oil. Add a spoonful of sugar and the slices of orange. Boil gently for 10 minutes and then simmer for 25 minutes until the sauce is thick. Take out the garlic if you must before serving.

Chaud-froid Sauce for Fish/Game
1 pt fish stock, 1 pt cream, ½ tsp. fresh tarragon (¼ pinch if dried), ½ oz. gelatine melted in a glass of white wine, salt, pepper (white). Substitute game stock and thyme or marjoram for game.

Reduce the mixture of stock and cream with the tarragon to 1½ pts by simmering. Stir in the wine and gelatine and heat gently. Adjust the seasoning. Stir the mixture in a basin over some ice until it begins to set. Then coat the fish with it.

Cherry Sauce for all Game

½ lb. cherries, 1 glass red wine, 3 tbs. sugar, ½ pt water, juice ½ lemon, pinch of cinnamon, 1 tsp. cornflour.

Soak the pitted cherries in the red wine, cook them gently for 20 minutes until they are soft, add the lemon juice, cinnamon, and sieve, or purée in a blender. Return to the saucepan and thicken with cornflour paste. Serve hot.

Colbert Butter

This is made from maître d'hôtel butter (see p. 171) with the addition of melted meat or fish glaze. Use 1 dessertspoon of the glaze to ¼ lb. maître d'hôtel butter.

Cream Sauce

This is made by adding double cream to béchamel sauce (see p. 166). 4 tbs. cream, ½ pt béchamel sauce.

Cumberland Sauce for Venison, Hare and Boar

Zest and juice of an orange and a lemon cut into very thin strips, 4 tbs. red-currant jelly, ½ small wine glass of port, pinch of mustard powder, and pepper.

Put the strips of orange and lemon into a pan with water to cover; boil, and drain off the water. Melt the jelly in a small pan and add the rest of the ingredients and the strips of orange and lemon before serving.

Sauce Diable for Venison etc.

An espagnole (brown, see p. 169) sauce to which chopped shallot, reduced wine vinegar, and tomato purée with Worcester sauce and a pinch of cayenne pepper are added.

½ cup wine vinegar reduced by one third, 1 tbs. chopped shallot, 1 cup espagnole sauce, 2 tbs. tomato purée, 1 tbs. Worcester sauce, pinch of cayenne pepper.

Egg and Lemon Sauce for Fish and Rabbit

1 pt rich fish stock, 3 beaten egg yolks, 1 lemon juice and rind, pepper, salt.

Put the fish stock into the double boiler (or substitute) and bring to the boil; (if the fish stock needs reducing, cook fiercely for 10 minutes and then let it simmer to evaporate to the required quantity). Move the saucepan away from the heat. Add the grated lemon rind and juice. Spoon the warm stock little by little into the beaten egg. Return the mixture to the double boiler and simmer until the mixture thickens to a thin custard-like consistency. Add pepper and salt if necessary.

Espagnole Sauce, a rich brown sauce

1 oz. butter, 1 oz. chopped streaky bacon, 1 chopped shallot, 2 large mushrooms chopped, 1 chopped carrot, 2 tbs. flour, ½ pt beef stock, bouquet garni, salt, pepper.

First fry the bacon in the butter for 3 minutes, add the vegetables and fry for another 3 minutes. Stir the flour in mixing it with the other ingredients until it is well browned. Reduce the heat and gradually add the stock to blend smoothly as the sauce thickens. Put in the bouquet, salt and pepper and allow the sauce to simmer for an hour over a very low heat. Stir occasionally to prevent the sauce sticking to the pan. Strain the sauce, pushing the solids through the sieve with a wooden spoon, and spoon off any excess fat. Adjust seasoning. It can be reheated when needed and added to other sauces as needed. In a covered jar the sauce will keep in a refrigerator for several days.

Sauce Grand Veneur for Venison

This is made by adding 1 tablespoon of gooseberry jelly to 1 cup of poivrade sauce (see p. 172).

Sauce Gribiche for cold Fish, au bleu or poached

3 whites and 3 yolks of hard-boiled eggs, 1 tsp. French mustard, salt, pepper, 1 tsp. vinegar, 2 tbs. olive oil, 2 chopped gherkins, 1 tbs. chopped parsley and capers.

Pound the ingredients together to a smooth paste, add the chopped herbs and the egg whites cut into fine strips.

Hollandaise Sauce

This is an emulsion of eggs and fat, but instead of olive oil butter is used; make it in a double boiler or improvised bain-marie.
2 tbs. wine vinegar, pinch white pepper, 4 tbs. water (or court bouillon when the sauce is for fish), 3 egg yolks, 6 ozs. butter (preferably unsalted), salt, 2 tsp. lemon juice.

Reduce the vinegar and water or stock to a third in a double boiler. Beat in the egg yolks gradually over a very low fire until they begin to thicken. Add the butter in tiny pieces one by one stirring all the time. Adjust seasoning and add lemon juice.

Horseradish Sauce

1 stick horseradish (or 2 tbs. ready prepared), white wine vinegar, 1 tsp. caster sugar, 4 tbs. thick cream, pepper (for prepared horseradish), salt.

Grate a stick of scrubbed and scraped horseradish. Add enough white vinegar just to cover and a teaspoon of caster sugar. Combine this with 4 tbs. thick cream, a pinch of pepper and a little salt.

Horseradish and Beetroot Sauce for Fish and Meat

1 or 2 sticks horseradish (or 4 tbs. prepared), 1 or 2 small beetroot, 1 tbs. acetic acid or wine vinegar.

Grate 3 tbs. of fresh horseradish and the peeled uncooked beetroot, add 1 tbs. acetic acid or wine vinegar, salt and pepper. If the horseradish is too strong add more beetroot or use the kind sold in jars.

Madeira Sauce

Add 3–4 tbs. Madeira to 1 pint of brown sauce (espagnole) to make Madeira sauce.

Maître d'Hôtel Butter

A heaped tablespoon of finely chopped parsley, lemon juice, salt and pepper added to 1 oz. butter.

Mayonnaise

This is an emulsion of egg yolks, olive oil flavoured with vinegar, mustard, pepper and salt.
2 egg yolks, 1 tsp. strong French mustard (Dijon), pinch of salt and pepper, 1 tsp. vinegar, ½ pt olive oil.

Put the egg yolks with the salt, pepper etc. into a heavy bowl and mix them together. Add, to start with, the olive oil drop by drop. When the eggs and oil have started to become a smooth mixture, the oil can be added in a very thin stream. The mixture must be stirred all the time the oil is being added. When all the oil has been added, it should be almost solid in consistency. Dilute it with a few drops of vinegar. If the mixture curdles it is because the oil is being poured in too fast. To put this right, start again with a spoonful of mustard in the bowl, and add the curdled mayonnaise very gradually indeed. With a large quantity it will be necessary to start with an egg yolk as well. To keep mayonnaise in a refrigerator add 2 tablespoons of boiling water – put it in a jar and cover tightly. Some cooks add the boiling water anyway, as it gives the mayonnaise a lighter texture.

Mornay Sauce for Fish

¾ pt béchamel sauce (see p. 166), ⅓ cup cream, 2 egg yolks, 2 oz. grated parmesan cheese, 3 tbs. fish stock, salt, pepper.

Add the ingredients to the hot béchamel sauce and cook for 2 minutes. Adjust seasoning before serving.

Nantua Sauce

¾ pt béchamel sauce (see p. 166), 2 oz. butter pounded with some shrimps, prawns or lobster, salt, pepper, 4 tbs. cream.

GARNISH

2 tbs. chopped shellfish.

Add the cream to the hot béchamel sauce, stirring well, and strain through a fine sieve. Season with salt and pepper and stir in the fish-flavoured butter and if available, the shellfish.

Sauce Niçoise

2 tbs. tomato purée, 1 sweet pepper (pimento), pinch chopped tarragon.

Mayonnaise (see above) with very thick tomato purée; pounded sweet pepper and chopped tarragon added; to ½ pt mayonnaise add 4 tablespoons of the purée.

Sauce Périgueux

½ pt rich meat stock, 2 tbs. Madeira, 2 tbs. chopped truffles.

Reduce to about a third the stock, add the Madeira and finally lower the heat to a point where the sauce is still very hot but not boiling and add the truffles.

Sauce Piquante

2 chopped shallots, bouquet garni, 3 tbs. wine vinegar, 1 cup stock, brown roux, black pepper, 1 tbs. mixture of chopped gherkin, capers and parsley.

Reduce the vinegar with the shallots and bouquet to one third. Add stock or gravy. Thicken with a brown roux. Cook for 5 minutes and add the gherkins, capers, parsley and freshly ground black pepper.

Sauce Poivrade, especially good with Venison

1 chopped carrot, onion, shallot, 1 bay leaf, sprig of thyme, or pinch if dried, salt, pepper, 2 tsp. flour, 1 oz. butter, ½ glass white or red wine, 1 tbs. vinegar, 1 cup rich meat stock.

Put the vegetables, bay leaf, thyme, salt and pepper, into a pan with the butter and cook gently, stirring all the time. When the mixture is brown and the vegetables are soft, sprinkle the flour onto it. Pour in the wine and vinegar gradually blending it with the flour, add stock. Simmer gently for ½ hour. Add more pepper for a really hot sauce, strain through a sieve before serving. This sauce can be varied by adding chopped ham, or some sauce espagnole.

Sauce Tartare

Finely chopped herbs, e.g. tarragon, chives, and parsley as well as capers and gherkins are added to mayonnaise to make sauce tartare.

Tomato Sauce

1 lb. coarsely chopped tomatoes, 1 onion or shallot finely chopped, 1 oz. butter, 1 tbs. olive oil, salt, pepper, 1 tsp. sugar, 1 finely chopped clove garlic; pinch dried basil, 1 tsp. chopped parsley.

Melt the onion in the oil and butter in a small heavy saucepan. Add salt, pepper and sugar, the tomatoes and herbs and cook gently until the sauce is thick but just runny.

Velouté Sauce for Fish

This is a sauce made from fish stock or jelly added to and thickened by a white roux. A velouté with white wine is a sauce vin blanc. 1 oz. butter, 1 oz. flour, ½ pt fish stock (seasoning if necessary).

Sauce Verte for Fish especially

This is made by adding watercress, tarragon, spinach and parsley to mayonnaise.
¾ pt mayonnaise (see p. 171), 10 sprigs watercress, 3 sprigs tarragon, 4 sprigs parsley, 10 leaves spinach.

Blanch the leaves only of the herbs and spinach. Strain all water off, pound them into a smooth paste. Sieve the paste into a bowl and mix this into the mayonnaise just before serving.

White Sauce

See p. 24.

Red Wine Sauce for Fish

Reduce the fish stock made with a red wine bouillon and add fresh butter, mixing it in little by little with a wooden spoon. In the case of fish braised in a red wine stock, add the braising liquid. A quarter teaspoon of anchovy essence may also be added. Remove fat from the braising liquid either by letting it set and taking off the fat from the top or spooning it off if it is to be used still hot. An ounce of butter to a pint of stock is a reasonable proportion.

White Wine Sauce

A reduced mixture of white wine, fish stock and mushrooms added to a velouté sauce (see p. 173) finished with beaten egg yolks and pea-sized pieces of butter.

2 cups reduced (see p. 21) white wine, 1 pt fish stock, 2 oz. chopped mushrooms, ½ cup velouté sauce, 1 beaten egg yolk, 1 oz. butter, 1 oz. flour.

INDEX